The Modern Eagle Guide

The F-15 Eagle/Strike Eagle Exposed

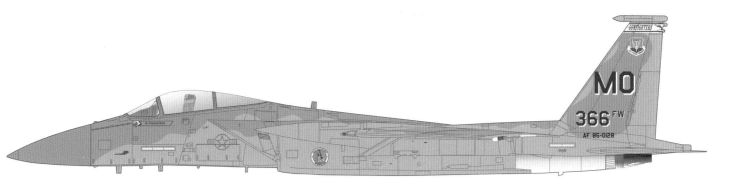

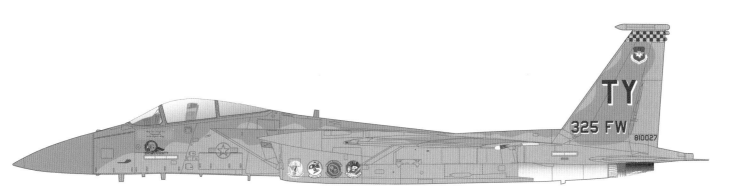

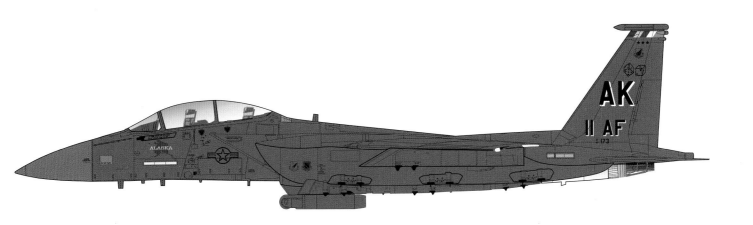

REID AIR PUBLICATIONS
The #1 Source for Modern Military Aviation Books

Jake Melampy

Reid Air Publications, LLC
1582 Haworth Court
Lebanon, Ohio 45036

First edition 2008

ISBN 978-0-9795064-4-4

Book layout and design by Jake Melampy

All photographs by author unless otherwise stated.

Acknowledgements
I would like to give special thanks to SSgt. Jasmine Reif (366th Fighter Wing), Maj. Damien Pickart (366th Fighter Wing), TSgt. Chris Holmes (4th Fighter Wing), Sgt. Mike Nickerson (102nd Fighter Wing), TSgt. Chris Boehlein (131st Fighter Wing), MSgt. Kevin Williams and the airmen of the F-15 MRA (362nd Training Squadron), Dave Whalen (F-15 Crewchief, retired), Zach Falzon, Greg Feiser, Ken Middleton, Darren "Motty" Mottram, and Dave Roof for their help with this book. Without their time, photos, or technical expertise, this book would not have been possible. A debt of gratitude is owed to Scott Brown and Geoff Martin of Afterburner Decals for allowing use of their artwork. All F-15 profile drawings are their work.

On the cover: A 4-ship of Missouri Air National Guard Eagles lines up for the camera. The sheer size of the Eagle is evident when compared to its pilot.

Title Page: Throughout the Eagle's career, many fighter squadrons in the USAF have operated the F-15. From top to bottom, F-15C 85-0128 of the 366th Fighter Wing, Mountain Home AFB, ID; F-15C 81-0027 of the 325th Fighter Wing, Tyndall AFB, FL; and F-15E 87-0173 of the 3rd Wing, Elmendorf AFB, AK. The latter two machines are from Wings seeing their Eagle fleet shrinking due to the introduction of the F-22A into USAF service.

Right: Although currently scheduled to begin losing their Eagles in late 2008, the 131st Fighter Wing continues to patrol the skies looking for potential trouble.

With a lifetime air-air kill record of 102-0, the Boeing F-15 Eagle reigns supreme as the most effective and lethal combat aircraft in the history of air warfare. Soon after its debut in July 1972, the Israeli Air Defense Force/Air Force (ADF/AF) bloodied its claws in the skies over Syria in 1979. Even now, as the Eagle approaches its 40th birthday, it is still widely regarded as one of the finest jet fighters in the sky.

The F-15 Eagle was conceived as a replacement for the wildly successful McDonnell-Douglas F-4 Phantom II in the early 1970's. The Phantom's record in Vietnam, while successful, made it clear to USAF planners that a new airframe was needed. The new airframe had to be designed with air superiority in mind from the very beginning.

The Eagle's recipe for success centers around its high-thrust engines that result in a very high thrust-to-weight ratio. This allows the jet to accelerate very quickly. In addition, excellent maneuverability is achieved via very large surface wing area and its resultant low wing-loading. This package, coupled with superior avionics and radar, long range, and an effective weapons suite, has proven to be a difficult-to-beat combination.

The Eagle first entered service with the United States Air Force at Luke AFB, Arizona, in 1974. The first Eagles arrived to establish the F-15 training program with the 58th Tactical Training Wing, while the first "combat" Eagles were delivered to the 1st Fighter Wing at Langley AFB, Virginia, in 1976. These initial deliveries were all comprised of the F-15A and two-seat F-15B.

Early Eagles were powered by the Pratt & Whitney F-100-PW-100 turbofan engines, rated at 23, 830 lbs. thrust in afterburner. These early engines, however, had a troubled beginning. High Angle of Attack (AOA) maneuvers often resulted in engine flameout. Overheating in the engines' turbine sections was also a frequent problem. Many of these problems were fixed as the experience with the engines grew and maintenance procedures were adapted.

The avionics suite in the Eagle was the most sophisticated ever installed in any jet fighter of the time. The F-15 was among the first to have true "HOTAS" (Hands On Throttle And Stick) capabilities, allowing the pilot to make changes to the radar, avionics, weapons system, etc, without removing his hands from the control stick or throttle. Similarly, its sophisticated HUD allowed the pilot to keep his eyes outside of the jet's canopy at all times.

The Hughes AN/APG-63 radar assembly was chosen to equip the Eagle fleet. This radar was designed specifically for the F-15, and represented massive leaps in technology and usefulness when compared to other, earlier, designs. It is tied into the HUD, which displays a diamond shape over the target's location, enabling the pilot to find his targets much more quickly than before. The radar offered several modes of search and Auto-Acquisition, enabling the pilot to select the mode that best suited the situation.

To protect itself from enemy aircraft and anti-aircraft artillery, the F-15 was equipped with a very sophisticated electronic warfare suite, known as TEWS (Tactical Electronic Warfare System), consisting of an AN/ALR-56 radar warning receiver, AN/ALQ-128 Electronic Warfare Warning System (EWWS), and AN/ALQ-135 Internal Counter Measures Set (ICMS, although this was not installed on the F-15B/D due to lack of space). Together, the TEWS components provide the pilot with warning and protection from various air- and ground-based radar threats, mostly without any direct assistance from the pilot.

The upgraded F-15C/D model appeared in 1979, and made its way into operational squadrons soon after. The F-15C boasted a slightly larger internal fuel capacity and the ability to carry FAST (Fuel And Sensor Tactical) packs. These were a precursor to the modern-day CFTs mounted on the F-15E, but lacked the integral air-ground weapons stations. They, did, however boost the Eagle's fuel capacity, and added the ability to carry various sensors and antenna. They retained the Sparrow missile rails, allowing the F-15C/D to retain its full air-air capability. The FAST packs were used in only a few instances, however, most notably with the 57th Fighter Interceptor Group, which held an alert assignment at Keflavik AB, Iceland. The increased fuel capacity of the F-15C resulted in a heavier gross weight of that aircraft. Consequently, the landing gear, including the tires, wheels, and brakes, were made stronger to handle the increased weight.

The biggest change to the F-15C is in that jet's electronics suite. The AN/APG-63 of the F-15C is greatly upgraded over the item found on the F-15A. The improved radar has a new Programmable Signal Processor (PSP) to allow quicker switching through the radar's various modes. Later, many F-15C/D models were equipped with the more reliable F100-PW-220 engines. This helped alleviate many of the problems associated with the older -100 engines. To further increase reliability and reduce maintenance, the engines' "turkey feathers" were removed, revealing the actuator rods. The increased drag that resulted was deemed a small price to pay for the reduced maintenance workload.

MSIP (Multi-Stage Improvement Program) introduced another significant improvement to the AN/APG-63, this time improving the computer's memory capability and processing speed. Other MSIP improvements were the installation of the Programmable Armament Control Set (PACS), upgraded TEWS/ECM gear, wiring to fire the new AIM-120 AMRAAM medium range missile, improved UHF radios, and integration of the F-15 with GPS systems. MSIP was first introduced to the F-15C late during the jet's production run. Earlier jets, including the F-15A/B, were retrofitted with many of these improvements. MSIP jets can be externally identified by a new antenna on the rear of the right side tailboom, adjacent to the horizontal stabilizer. In the cockpit, a new Multi-Purpose Color Display (MPCD) was added in place of the original Armament Control Panel along with a new control stick grip.

A similar upgrade program, known as MSIP II, took place beginning in 1985. It added the new AN/APG-70 radar that nearly doubled processor memory. Again, many earlier jets were retrofitted with the new equipment. The program was completed by the early 1990s.

The first production F-15E rolled off the assembly line at St. Louis in November 1986, making its first flight the following month. Although the Strike Eagle is externally similar in appearance to the "light grey" F-15A-D, it is essentially an all-new machine. The airframe is stressed to allow a 16,000 hour lifespan, nearly double that of the "light greys". It is also built to withstand the Strike Eagle's increased weight.

The F-15E's electronics suite centers around the AN/APG-70 radar. The radar retains its full air-air capabilities, but is also optimized for the Strike Eagle's air-ground task. Potential targets can be identified by as much as 100 miles away.

LANTIRN (Low Altitude Navigation and Targeting, Infra-Red for Night) is a two-podded system to give the F-15E a true night/precision capability. LANTIRN consists of two pods, one each slung beneath the jet's intakes on special adaptor pylons. The AN/AAQ-13 navigation pod is mounted to the jet's right side. It contains a FLIR (Forward-Looking Infra-Red), used to display a video image of the surrounding terrain on the pilot's HUD, allowing him to fly at night at low altitudes. The nav pod also contains a terrain-following radar effective in poor weather. The jet's autopilot system can be tied into the nav pod to enable the jet to fly without pilot input as low as 200 feet above the ground. Under the jet's left intake is the AN/AAQ-14 targeting pod. The AAQ-14 contains a high-resolution tracking FLIR and a laser designator, used to steer laser-guided weapons onto their targets using reflected laser light.

Both front and rear cockpits are new designs, relying on digital instruments and Multi-Purpose Displays (MPDs). The forward station is reserved for the pilot. A new, F-15E-specific HUD is present, as are three MPDs for navigation, weapons delivery, and aircraft systems information. A dedicated Weapons Systems Officer (WSO) occupies the rear cockpit. His station is loaded with four MPDs and a pair of control sticks to steer the targeting pod and radar onto targets.

The Strike Eagle is fitted with Conformal Fuel Tanks, complete with integral weapons stations to increase the jet's air-ground load. The F-15E retains the M61A1 20mm cannon, although the ammunition capacity is reduced. The Strike Eagle also retains full air-air capability, including the four Sparrow launchers built into the bottom of the CFT pylons. Additionally, a new TEWS system is installed. The antenna for this system is flush-mounted on the Strike Eagle, replacing blade antenna found on the "Light Grey" jets.

Initial Strike Eagles were fitted with the same -220 powerplant as the "light grey" jets. However, the increased weight of the Strike Eagle resulted in the installation of the new F100-PW-229 Increased Performance Engine. The first F-15E so fitted was F-15E 90-0233. All subsequent jets have the -229 engines as standard equipment.

The F-15 has had a successful foreign campaign to equip friendly nations with the jet for use with their air forces. To date, Israel and Saudi Arabia have ordered the F-15A/B/C/D (although only F-15C/D for Saudi Arabia). Both nations have used their Eagles in combat with success. These jets differ little from USAF versions with the exception of slightly downgraded avionics and ECM suites. The Japanese Air Self Defense Force (JASDF) has gone a step further and received licensing from Boeing to manufacture the Eagle in Japan. The aircraft are known as F-15J (F-15DJ for the two-seat versions).

In an effort to keep the F-15 production line open, Boeing undertook an aggressive marketing campaign to persuade friendly countries to purchase the F-15E. This campaign has resulted in the F-15I for Israel, F-15S for Saudi Arabia, F-15SG for the Republic of Singapore, and F-15K for South Korea, all modified from the F-15E. These jets are very similar to USAF versions of the F-15E, but again delivered without the full ECM suite and downgraded radar. The F-15K, however, is perhaps the most advanced Eagle to patrol the skies of any version. It retains its ALQ-128 and ALQ-135 ICMS/ECM equipment. Additionally, the Koreans have opted for the General Electric F110-GE-129 engines to provide thrust for the F-15K, as have the Republic of Singapore for their F-15SG.

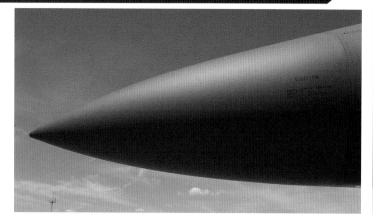

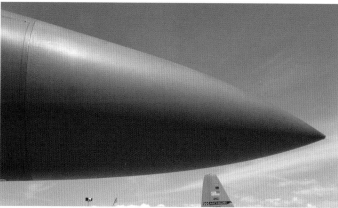

The sole job of the radome of the F-15 is to provide an aerodynamic cover over the jet's radar assembly, while at the same time allowing the radar to "see" through it. The radome is constructed of a composite material. The radome of the F-15E, above left and above right, is identical to other F-15s, but lacks the urethane boot on the forward tip, visible on the "light grey" F-15's radome, right and below. The urethane boot serves as a reinforcement to the radome. Some early radomes were prone to cracking and delamination in this area, which the urethane boot helps prevent. However, the newer radomes found on the F-15E were strengthened internally, negating the need for the urethane boot. It is sometimes possible to find a replacement radome, without the urethane boot, present on the fighter F-15 versions. A screw and metal cap, bottom, is present on the forward tip of all F-15 radomes. It is the manufacturing point from the factory, and serves no purpose once the radome is delivered to the fighter squadron. It is worth pointing out that in many cases, the color of the radome does not match the color of the surrounding camouflage of the jet. Radomes are not repainted along with the rest of the jet during a normal re-paint. They are covered with a special coating, and are only re-coated at depot-level maintenance. F-15E radomes can be fitted to F-15A/B/C/D models, but not vice versa.

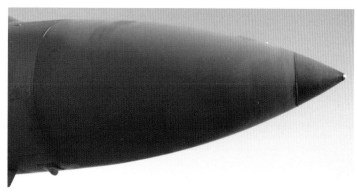

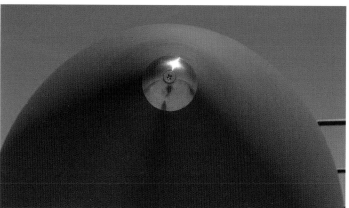

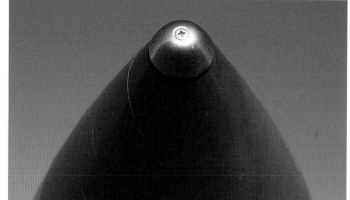

Jake Melampy

The Eagle is fitted with either the Raytheon (formerly Hughes Aviation) AN/APG-63 or AN/APG-70 radar system. These radar assemblies are pulse-doppler radar systems designed with both air-air and air-ground missions in mind. They perform equally well when looking up at high-altitude targets or looking down at low-altitude targets without being confused by ground clutter. The radar can detect and track aircraft and small high-speed targets at distances beyond visual range (BVR) down to close range, and at altitudes down to the treetops. The radar feeds target information into the aircraft's central weapons computers for effective weapons delivery. For close-range dogfights, the radar automatically acquires enemy aircraft and projects target/location information onto the cockpit's HUD (Heads Up Display).

The Hughes Aviation AN/APG-63 radar assembly was the unit initially fitted to all F-15 A and B models, as well as early F-15C/D models. This radar combines long range acquisition and attack capabilities with automatic features to provide the instant information and computations required during air-to-air and air-to-surface engagements.

The AN/APG-70 is very similar to the AN/APG-63, but vastly improved in many areas. The AN/APG-70 features new air-to-air and air-to-surface modes allowing ground attack capability. It also offers greater reliability and less maintenance. It is installed in the F-15E, Saudi Arabia's F-15S, and Israel's F-15I aircraft.

The AN/APG-63(v1) radar is a reliability/maintainability hardware redesign which also provided significant mode growth opportunities. It was designed to replace outmoded APG-63 radars installed in the F-15 C/D models, providing improved performance and a dramatic increase in reliability. It was the first airborne radar system to incorporate a software programmable signal processor, allowing software upgrades without replacing hardware. The AN/APG-63(v1) is fitted to many, but not all, USAF F-15C/Ds. It is also fitted to South Korea's F-15K.

All the above radar assemblies have mechanically steered arrays (the radar dish). While upgrades over the years have improved them, the mechanical steering components are a point of potential failure given the amount of stresses put on them, and better radar technologies have appeared. The AN/APG-63(V)2 has been retrofitted to eighteen F-15Cs with the 3rd Wing at Elmendorf AFB, Alaska. This is an Active Electronically Scanned Array (AESA) radar upgrade that includes most of the new hardware from the APG-63(V)1, but adds an AESA to provide increased pilot situational awareness. Active Electronically-Scanned Array (AESA) radars are made of hundreds of thousands of small transmitter/receiver elements. Moving parts are eliminated; instead, subsets of their array elements are used to focus on each task very quickly and precisely, without having to move them physically, and with little signal "leakage" outside of its focused beams. This makes it more reliable, more powerful, and able to operate multiple modes at once. There's also a maintenance advantage. A partial failure in previous radars renders them unuseable, but AESA radars only suffer a slight performance drop if some of its modules fail. The AESA radar has an exceptionally agile beam, providing nearly instantaneous track updates and enhanced multi-target tracking capability. The APG-63(V)2 is compatible with current F-15C weapon loads and enables pilots to take full advantage of AIM-120 AMRAAM capabilities, simultaneously guiding multiple missiles to several targets widely spaced in azimuth, elevation, or range.

To gain access to the radome, four bolts need to be removed from inside the forward avionics bays. The radome hinges open to the jet's right side, then secured in place by a hinge lock bracket and a prop rod to prevent the radome from closing on the radar dish assembly. The hinge lock bracket and prop rod mount onto the bulkhead for easy stowage. The location of each of this is marked in black on the bulkhead. The hinge lock bracket stowage space is visible in the photo below. It is the black triangular shape.

USAF

The radar assembly consists of several individual components, of which the main radar dish is obviously the most prominent. It features ten IFF (Identify Friend or Foe) interrogators on the surface used to distinguish friendly aircraft vs. enemy aircraft well before the target can be visually identified. Behind the bulkhead, aft of the radar dish, are the remaining components of the radar. The power assembly, data processor, signal processor, transmitter, analog signal converter, and the receiver/exciter are all stored in the forward avionics bays immediately behind the radome (page 75).

Jake Melampy

The radar dish sweeps up, down, left, and right to find and track its targets. Hydraulic pressure from the jet's Utility system provides the power to do so. Although there are internal software and capability differences from one radar version to the next, all the radar assemblies remain identical externally.

Below-- The radome prop rod is visible at the bottom of the photo, as is the black triangular shape on the bulkhead to mark the stowage position of the radome hinge lock bracket. It is on the bulkhead's lower right corner below the radome hinge. The hinge allows the radome to close back into position. It, too, is plainly visible. With no hydraulic pressure available to the radar assembly, the dish sags towards the ground and requires assistance to reveal the area behind the dish.

Behind the radome is the upper ICMS (Internal Counter Measures System) AN/ALQ-135 Band 3 nodule. An identical Band 3 nodule is on the bottom of the jet, also behind the radome. These are a recent addition to the F-15, and not installed on all airframes. The Band 3 upgrade incorporates an improvement in capabilites and bandwith. They are only found on select F-15Cs from operational combat squadrons (as opposed to training squadrons). They are not found on the F-15A/B, nor the F-15D, as the two-seat versions (with the exception of the F-15E Strike Eagle) do not have any ECM gear installed due to lack of space. The ECM gear, including the ICMS, is located in Bay 5 behind the front cockpit of the F-15A/C. The addition of the rear cockpit in the F-15B/D made installation of ECM gear impossible.

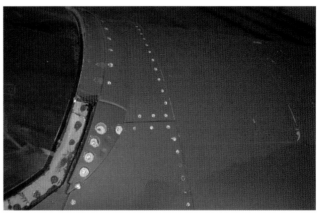

A flush-mounted EWWS (Electronic Warfare Warning System) antenna is located behind the AN/ALQ-135 Band 3 nodule. Two additional EWWS antennas are located on either side of the nose, forward of the pitots (see page 74). On some aircraft, these antenna are noticeably lighter than the surrounding paint, as shown above and below right. Others, however, are the same color, below left. To protect against ice formation and help clear rain away, a duct is located at the base of the windscreen, right. Engine bleed air is pumped through this vent to clear the windscreen of ice/rain.

Greg Fieser

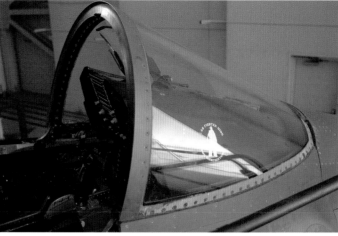

The Eagle pilot is afforded a near 360-degree view through the slightly bulged canopy. The windscreen is a one-piece, seamless piece constructed of formed plastic that is almost immune to birdstrikes. Ice/rain protection is provided via a vent, above, immediately forward of the windscreen. The vent, controlled by the windshield anti-ice switch in the cockpit, directs heated air from the jet's Environmental Control System (ECS) onto the windscreen to melt any ice that may be present.

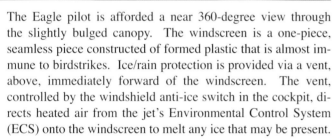

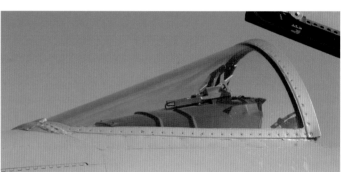

The two-seat Eagle canopy is larger and heavier than the single-seat canopy. All canopies, regardless of the Eagle version, use Utility hydraulic power, assisted by an air precharge, to raise and lower the canopy. The canopy actuators, located at the aft end of the canopy, have an air precharge on one side and hydraulic pressure on the other side. The air precharge makes it easier to lift the canopy, while the hydraulic side does the actual raising/lowering. Restrictions in the hydraulic power supply lines prevent the canopy from raising or lowering too quickly.

USAF

Greg Fieser

Three rear-view mirrors are mounted to the canopy bow (one at the 12 O'clock position and two at the 10 and 2 O'clock positions). In addition, a standby magnetic compass is adjacent to the center-mounted mirror. It is used as a back-up to the primary flight instruments in case of their failure. To the left of the center mirror is the air-refueling status light. This light is normally out, but illuminates when the refueling slipway door is opened and the air refueling system performs a successful self-test to determine it is ready for fuel. Once the light is on, the pilot may initiate the refueling process. The light goes out again once the tanker's boom is connected into the Eagle's refueling receptacle. The light re-illuminates when the tanker's boom disconnects from the F-15, and remains on until the refueling slipway door is closed.

Greg Fieser

Left and above-- Single-seat Eagles have an internal manual unlock handle mounted on the right canopy rail. A quick-release pin secures the handle in the locked position. The pilot lifts the handle up and back to manually raise the canopy. This handle is only found on the F-15A/C. It is not found on the F-15B/D/E models.

Below-- The canopy is aligned with the windscreen and fuselage to ensure a proper seal via four latches (ten on the two-seat canopies) on the canopy frame that engage rollers on the canopy sill. The latches also double as a means of locking the canopy in the closed position. The index pins in the forward edge of the canopy, below left, slide into matching holes in the windscreen, further ensuring a good fit and tight seal.

Greg Fieser

Jake Melampy

Internal Canopy structure

On many USAF F-15A-D models, the JHMCS (Joint Helmet-Mounted Cuing System) sensor is mounted on the left canopy rail. It works directly with the AIM-9X Sidewinder. It is only found on modern Eagles with AIM-9X capability. It is installed on two-seat F-15B/D models, but only for the front cockpit. At the time of this book's writing, it is slowly being introduced into the F-15E fleet.

Greg Fieser

The avionics bay behind the cockpit ("Bay 5") is covered by a flat panel built into the canopy framework of the F-15A/C. Bay 5 is not pressurized, unlike the remainder of the cockpit. Visible on the bottom of the canopy is the rubber canopy seal. Also visible at the rear of the canopy is the canopy actuator. It is shown a bit more closely in the bottom right photo. The coiled metal line is the canopy actuator initiator lanyard. During the ejection sequence, the canopy comes off of the jet, pulling the lanyard. The initiator then sends a signal to the recovery sequencer in the ejection seat telling it that the canopy is off and the seat is clear to eject. In the event of a signal failure, the seat will still eject, punching through the canopy with the help of canopy breakers on the top of the seat. At bottom left, the device behind the canopy strut is known as the "catcher's mitt". It receives the canopy remover during the ejection sequence to remove the canopy from the jet.

17

Greg Fieser

Greg Fieser

The forward part of the F-15B/D canopy is identical to that found on the single-seat F-15A/C. The exception is that the two-seat canopies (including the F-15E canopy, next page) lack the internal manual unlock handle mounted on the right canopy rail due to the increased weight of the two-seater's canopy. To raise the two-seater's canopy manually in the event of normal system failure, a hand-pump located on the right side of the nose wheel well is used to build sufficient hydraulic pressure.

Greg Fieser

Greg Fieser

Greg Fieser

Jake Melampy

The F-15E canopy is similar to that found on the F-15B/D, but has added ducting from the Environmental Control System (ECS) to help cool the Strike Eagle's additional avionics.

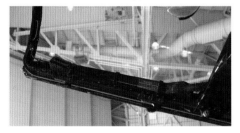

The forward framing is seen above (left side of the canopy frame) and below (right side of the frame). The increased ducting is readily apparent. The hook-shaped latches that align and lock the canopy are also visible.

The rear cockpit, too, has the additional ducting from the ECS. The aft left canopy rail is shown above, while the right side is below. Notice the "towel rack" handles on the aft canopy framing--something not found in the forward part of the canopy structure.

Eagle drivers have a largely unobstructed view through the windscreen, with only the HUD combining glass in the line of sight. The HUD (Heads-Up Display) dominates the top of the F-15's instrument panel glareshield. The pilot can look through the HUD at his target for the entire duration of the engagement, yet still have the vital information available to him without looking down at his flight instruments. Footage from the HUD is recorded for later playback during the pilots' debrief. Originally, the F-15A/B model had a primitive HUD recording system. The HUD film was a cartridge loaded onto the side of the HUD. The F-15C/D model introduced the 3/4" VTR (Video Tape Recorder, above) in the mid-1980's. The recorder was inside a door on the inboard side of the left intake. The pilots would bring a tape slightly bigger then a VHS tape to the Eagle's crewchief. The crewchief would insert the tape for the flight, then remove it after the sortie for the de-brief. The 3/4" VTR was also later installed on existing F-15A/B models. The VTR was modified in the late 1980's to accept a new 8mm tape compatible with the same camera. This is the 8mm AVTR (Airborne Video Tape Recorder), which is still in use today. The 8mm AVTR was a tremendous improvemet. It added full-color capability and a two hour capacity (vs. 30 minutes with the 3/4" VTR). The active-duty USAF (and export versions of the Eagle) use this system, shown below left. These aircraft use a custom-built camera mount that partially obscures the HUD optics, blocking some symbology on the HUD glass. To improve this, the Air National Guard modified the AVTR mount to a design of its own beginning in the early 1990's, shown below right, using the existing mount from the previous VTR system. Although the actual AVTR remained the same, the new mounting system alleviated the HUD optics interference problem, and had the added benefit of being far easier to maintain and adjust. However, to bring every jet up to the same standards, the USAF introduced a TCTO (Time-Compliant Technical Order) in the mid-1990s that ordered the ANG to adopt the USAF style AVTR mount. The TCTO had been completed by the late 1990's. Very few F-15C/D models that serve in the ANG received the modified mounting system.

On the top of the instrument panel's glareshield, to the left of the HUD glass, is the VSD (Vertical Situation Display) video camera mounting adapter. The camera slides down into position to capture the display on the VSD scope, which is almost directly below it on the main instrument panel. It is shown in detail on page 25.

In addition to the HUD and VSD cameras, a third camera was installed on all F-15A-Ds beginning in 2002. The MPCD (which is only found on post-MSIP aircraft, see next page) received a camera of its own to capture its display during the flight. It is mounted to the left side of the windscreen canopy rail, pointing down towards the MPCD. For the most part, it works well. However, pilots often complain that in bright, sunlit conditions, the picture is washed out from too much light.

The HUD control panel is under the Main Communications Control Panel (MCCP) at the top of the instrument panel. As its name implies, the MCCP allows the pilot to select radio frequencies and IFF transponder "squawk" codes. The MCCP has remained unchanged over the years. The VTR panel is mounted to the side of the HUD panel/MCCP. It has received minor changes over the years as the VTR has changed. The F-15A/B's MCCP is above and above right, leaving the F-15C/D MCCP below and below right.

The main instrument panel is conventional in design. The MCCP is at the top of the panel. It is flanked on either side by the VSD scope to the left, and the RWR (Radar Warning and Receiving) scope to the right. Below the MCCP are the primary flight instruments. The engine instruments are located on the right side of the panel below the RWR scope. The left side of the panel is home to the Armament Control Panel, which is the central control point for all of the Eagle's weapons. There is remarkably little difference in the cockpits over the years, and even between the F-15A and F-15C. At top left of the previous page is an early F-15A cockpit, with the layout as described above. Below left is a modern F-15A cockpit, after MSIP. The largest difference is the additon of a 6" MPCD (Multi-Purpose Control Display) which replaced the original Armament Control Panel. Also different, although not a result of MSIP, is the different style HUD camera, as discussed earlier. The top photo shows the original 3/4" VTR. The bottom photo shows the 8mm AVTR with the ANG-modified camera mounted to a 102nd Fighter Wing F-15A. The MPCD camera is also visible in this photo along the left-side windscreen bow. Contrast these two photos against the modern-day F-15C, right and above right. The F-15C is very similar to the late-model F-15A. The F-15C, although originally equipped with the same Armament Control Panel as that found on the F-15A, also has had the MPCD installed as a result of MSIP. The VSD camera mount is slightly different than that found on earlier jets. The HUD camera is the standard USAF-style 8mm AVTR, as this jet is assigned to the 390th Fighter Squadron at Mountain Home AFB, Idaho. This jet also has the MPCD camera installed.

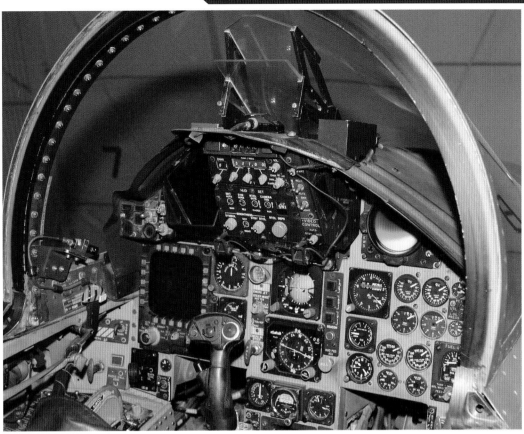

Greg Fieser

The left side of the instrument panel is dominated by the Armament Control Panel. This is the central point for all of the Eagle's air-air weaponry. The original panel is at left. To the right of this, from top to bottom, is the airspeed indicator, Angle of Attack indicator, and an accelerometer. The yellow/black handle on the canopy frame is the emergency canopy jettison lever. It is used to quickly blow the canopy off of the jet during a ground emergency. On the ground, it has a pin inserted into it to prevent accidental activation. The pin has a red streamer to increase visibility in the hopes of preventing flight with the pin still inserted into the lever.

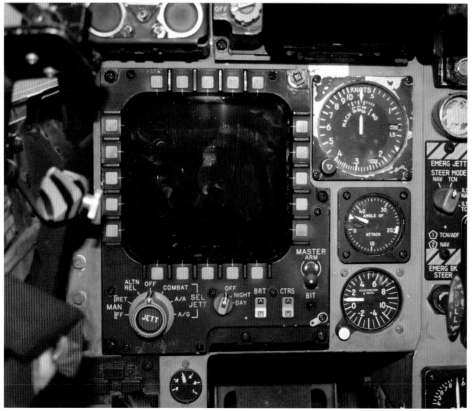

MSIP introduced a new Programmable Armament Control Set (PACS) in the mid-1980s, featuring a new Multi-Purpose Color Display (MPCD, left). This was initially fitted into the F-15C/D (including some still on the McDonnell Douglas assembly line), but also retrofitted into all existing F-15A/B models as well. The new system is a great advantage over the old, simply because it is digital vs. the old analog system. On the original Armament Control Panel, the pilot was required to enter the armament load information manually. Each window on the panel was individually entered prior to flight, which was very time consuming. The new PACS is able to recognize the weapons load as it is loaded onto the aircraft. No further action is required from the pilot. From a maintenance point of view, the PACS is also far easier to maintain and troubleshoot for the same reasons. Maintenance BIT (Built-In Test) testing now takes about ten minutes, a large difference from the 90 minutes required for the older system.

The VSD (Vertical Situation Display) is to the left of the MCCP. The VSD is also sometimes called the "Radar Scope." All radar data is displayed on the VSD, whereas the HUD displays only certain radar information. In addition, the jet's current INS coordinates and current date/time are displayed. A rubber "boot" surrounds the VSD to shield it from bright sunlight, making its display easier to read. Above the VSD, mounted on top of the instrument panel's glareshield, is the VSD camera mount. It "looks down" onto the VSD's flat screen. Using an angled mirror on the inside of the rubber boot, the VSD's display is "bounced" up into the camera mount to record everything the VSD displays during flight. The VSD camera is controlled by the small control panel to the left of the VSD.

Right-- The fire/overheat protection control panel is in the top left corner of the main panel, to the left of the VSD. It consists of three red lights to inform the pilot of a potential fire. With this panel, the pilot can identify a problem, then direct extinguishing agent into the problem area. The system can detect a fire situation in the forward and afterburner sections of each engine bay, as well as the engines' accessory drive and JFS. The extinguishing agent can be directed into these sensing element zones depending on the situation. The MPCD camera is in the foreground mounted to the windscreen rail.

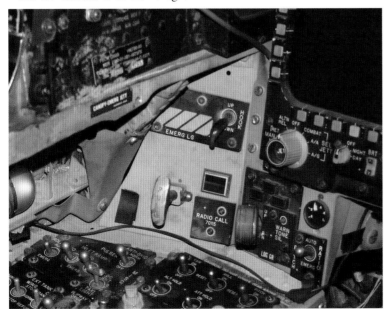

The lower left part of the panel is home to a few other miscellaneous controls. The landing gear handle and status lights are directly below the red emergency stores jettison button on the MPCD. The emergency arrestor hook handle is to the left of the red stores jettison button. Next to the landing gear handle is the Emergency Landing Gear handle. The Emergency Gear Extension system uses stored and pressurized hydraulic fluid from the JFS accumulator bottles to force the landing gear down as an alternative to the normal landing gear system. To the right of the gear handle is the Pitch Ratio Indicator and control switch. The Manual Flight Control system automatically adjusts the Pitch Ratio. It can vary from "0% to 100%" (0 to 1.0) This is dependant mainly upon airspeed, altitude and landing gear position. The switch can command the Pitch Ratio to either auto or Emergency modes. In Emergency mode, the Pitch Ratio is commanded to 40%.

Greg Fieser

The two primary flight instruments are conveniently located in the center of the instrument panel under the HUD control panel. The top instrument is the Attitude Director Indicator (ADI), giving the pilot pitch and roll information. Below that is the Horizontal Situation Indicator (HSI). This is provides heading, bearing, and navigation information to the pilot. These instruments are unchanged from the early F-15A, above left, late MSIP F-15A, above right, to the MSIP F-15C, right. The round yellow button to the left of the ADI is the Emergency Jettison button. When pushed, this jettisons all external stores, including external fuel tanks, to improve the jet's performance in an emergency. Below this is the Steer Mode switch. This controls the Flight Director information as displayed on the HSI and ADI. It can be set to either ILS or TACAN data. To the left of the HSI is the Emergency Brake/Steering handle. When pulled, this allows hydaulic pressure stored in the JFS accumulators to flow into the nosewheel steering unit on the landing gear to provide steering should the normal system fail to function properly. Simultaneously, it allows the same stored hydraulic pressure to flow to the main brakes to ensure sufficient braking.

Left--The rudder pedals are fully adjustable fore and aft to suit the pilot's needs. Each rudder has the McDonnell Douglas logo on it.

HUD mode switches are located to the right of the ADI and HSI. These three buttons dictate in which mode the HUD displays information (navigation mode vs. air-air, for example). The small grey knob below the HUD mode switches is the rudder pedal adjustment knob.

Rounding out the instrument panel is a look at the right side of the panel. At the top right of the panel, adjacent to the MCCP and HUD control panel, is the RWR/TEWS (Tactical Electronic Warfare System) scope. The TEWS scope displays potential threats to the jet as detected by the F-15's RWR (Radar Warning Receiver) gear. Below this is the remainder of the flight, engine, hydraulic, and fuel instruments. The altimeter is the largest of these. It is placed below the TEWS scope. Below that is the Vertical Velocity Indicator (VVI), which displays the rate at which the jet is climbing/descending. Next is the standard 8-day clock, beneath the VVI. The engine instruments are to the right of the three flight instruments. There are two of each, simply because there are two engines on the F-15. At top, to the right of the altimeter, are the engine percent RPM gauges that display the engines' speed. Below these is the pair of FTIT (Fan Turbine Inlet Temperature) instruments, followed by the Fuel Flow Indicators. The bottom two engine instruments are the engines' exhaust nozzle indicators, which read the amount the nozzles are opened. At the top right of the panel is the hydraulic system monitoring instruments. The Eagle has three separate hydraulic systems (PC1, PC2, and Utility, as discussed on page 114). Each of these systems has its own pressure gauge. Below this is the engine oil pressure instruments.

The pilot is kept aware of the Eagle's fuel condition by a single display in the lower right corner of the panel, to the right of the engine exhaust nozzle position indicators. This single display reads the amount of fuel in each of the F-15's fuel tanks, including any external drop tanks, when carried. Below this is the Jet Fuel Starter (JFS) activation handle. The pilot pulls this to start the JFS prior to engine start. To the right of this is the cabin pressure altimeter. A bank of warning/caution indicator lights is on the right edge of the panel. These illuminate to notify the pilot of a system malfunction or other kind of potential problem. The small handle to the right of this is the Emergency Vent Handle used to quickly dump cabin pressure in the event of cabin over-

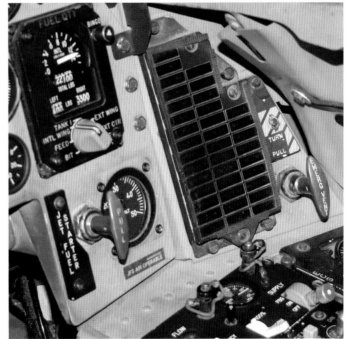

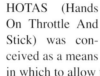

HOTAS (Hands On Throttle And Stick) was conceived as a means in which to allow the pilot to devote as much time as possible looking outside the Eagle's canopy during a fight. Switches are placed on the throttles and control stick to enable the pilot to make changes and/or adjustments to the radar, designate a target, or select weapons without removing his hands from the controls. Two throttles, above and left, are located on the left side panel. Either can be manipulated independently of the other. The throttles are moved forward to increase thrust on the engines. Full afterburner is at the furthest point forward in the throttles' travel. The brushes in the throttle tracks prevent foreign objects from falling into the tracks. As the name implies, the Friction Lever adjusts the amount of friction to the throttles as they are moved throughout their travel, requiring more or less force to make adjustments as the pilot's preferences dictate. The control stick, below, has had some changes made to it over the years. Below left is the original stick installed in all F-15A/B/C/D models from the factory. This stick gave way to a new design in the early 1990s that adds additional controls, below center and below right.

Greg Fieser

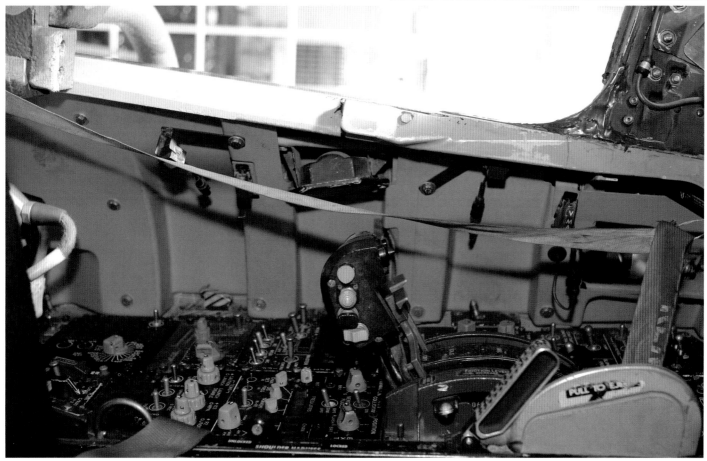

For the most part, the sidewalls of the Eagle are relatively simple and not too cluttered. They are certainly less cluttered than earlier McDonnell Douglas aircraft such as the F-4. On the jet's left side, above, only a handful of switches are on the side. The yellow ribbon leads from the Emergency Canopy Jettison lever (page 24) back to the canopy-actuated initiator lanyard in Bay 5 (page 37). On the jet's right side, below, things are slightly busier. The canopy control handle, inset right, is located at the top of the sidewall. It is the pilot's primary method of raising or lowering the canopy. The mass of wiring on this side is NVIS (Night VISion) lighting. It is extends up to the MCCP. It was added recently, and not present on earlier jets.

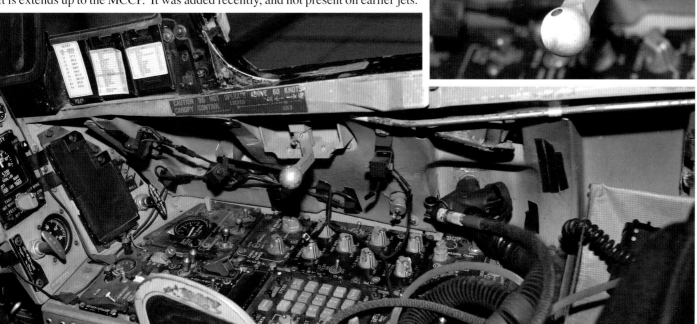

Greg Fieser

The throttle quadrant is located on the left side instrument panel console, taking up a large amount of space next to the pilot. The remainder of the left side panel is allotted to the communications panel, fuel management panel, external aircraft lighting panel, autopilot control, ILS/TACAN, IFF, and radar control panels. A BIT panel is located at the rear end for testing the jet's avionics. The yellow/black striped guarded switch is the emergency air refueling slipway control. Few changes have taken place to the side panel over the years. The BIT panel has changed location, and a few of the panels have had slight alterations as new equipment has been added to the Eagle's inventory. The top photo of the previous page depicts a pre-MSIP

F-15A. It has a noticeably more worn appearance than the modern-day MSIP F-15C at the bottom of the previous page, and above.

The pilot's G-suit connects to a fitting at the aft end of the left side panel, above and right. Air is provided courtesy of the heat exchanger. This particular aircraft above right has a plastic bag placed over the G-suit fitting to prevent foreign object entry during maintenance.

31

Greg Fieser

The right side instrument panel is home to many of the aircraft's systems controls. The oxygen system, anti-ice system, cabin temperature, cockpit lighting, ECM and TEWS gear, and the jet's navigation system can all be managed from this side of the cockpit. This panel has remained virtually unchanged from the beginning of the Eagle's life up to and including the modern jet. On the previous page, an early F-15A panel is shown at top, followed by a modern MSIP F-15A in the center, and a modern MSIP F-15C on the bottom.

The tubing that connects to the rear half of the panel is the pilot's oxygen supply hoses and microphone cord. The largest ribbed hose leads to the Liquid Oxygen tank in the forward fuselage. This provides normal breathing oxygen for the pilot during flight. The black fitting at the end of this hose mates with the pilot's oxygen mask's hose, then slips into a bracket on the pilot's survival vest. The smaller hose that is connected to the black fitting at the end of the oxygen hose is the emergency oxygen supply. This hose leads from the green emergency oxygen bottle mounted to the side of the ejection seat. In the event of a high-altitude ejection, this bottle will provide limited breathing oxygen until the pilot descends to a lower altitude. The third hose, strapped to the ribbed oxygen hose, is the pilot's microphone cord. This, too, connects to the pilot's oxygen mask to allow the pilot to speak on the radio or intercom.

Chris Boehlein

A map case is provided at the aft end of the panel, against the rear bulkhead. This is used for stowage of various items, from charts, approach plates, water bottles, etc. The map case has also been home to the AVTR and related components. The Air National Guard opted to locate the AVTR tape deck and CCU (Camera Control Unit) here to simplify maintenance, right. The actual camera, however, remains in front of the HUD glass, obviously. A movable map light is clamped onto the map case. It can be located virtually anywhere using its alligator clips. Notice the amount of chipping on the cockpit sill below.

Greg Fieser

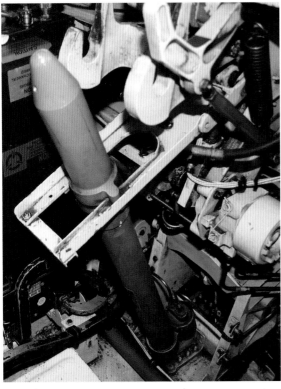

Bay 5 is located behind the cockpit in the F-15A and F-15C. Many electrical components, relays, wire bundles, and avionics are stored in this area. In addition, all of the aircraft's TEWS and ICMS equipment is stored in racks along the bay's left side. Aircraft built in 1979 and earlier have a metallic green bay. However, the color was changed to white beginning with 1980 machines, and continuing until the end of F-15C production in 1986. The forward wall of the bay, behind the ejection seat, houses the canopy remover. This torpedo-shaped device contains a pyrotechnic charge in its base. At the beginning of the ejection sequence, the charge fires, forcing the canopy remover into the bowl-shaped "catcher's mitt" on the bottom of the canopy framing (page 17), physically removing the canopy from the jet. The small white box in the upper right corner is an electrical voltage regulator.

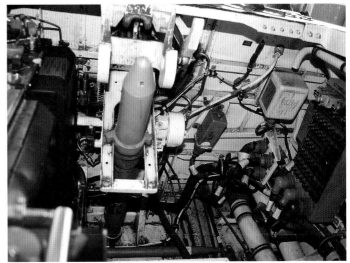

The right side of the bay is crammed full of electrical components. At the front of the right wall is a circuit breaker panel. Behind it, the four black boxes are the Anti-Skid brake fault indicator box (the largest box), external lighting flasher control (to the right of the brake control), and two overheat detectors (the two smallest boxes above the lighting flasher control). Three large relay boxes are behind the control boxes, followed by another circuit breaker panel. The three small boxes at the rear of the side wall are more relay boxes. The relay boxes and circuit breaker panels regulate a wide variety of systems throughout the aircraft. Also present along the lower side wall, and in fact the entire Bay 5, is a large amount of wiring bundles and harnesses. The two large pipes on the floor of the bay are bleed air pipes leading from the Heat Exchanger to the avionics bays used for cooling of the avionics in these bays.

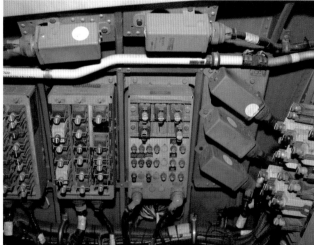

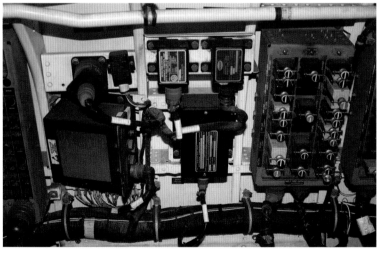

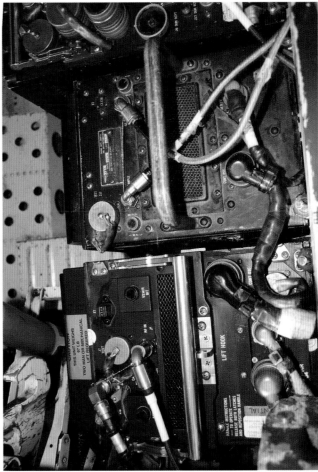

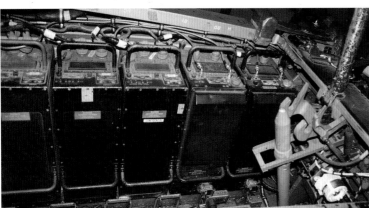

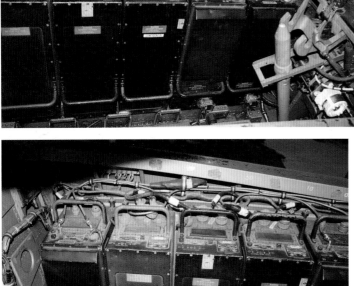

The Eagle's ICMS (Internal Counter Measures System) components are lined up against the left wall. Each box is surprisingly heavy; placards are placed in several places on each box warning of its heavy weight. The Eagle's ICMS has received several upgrades over the years to keep pace with technology. As a result, the individual boxes in Bay 5 have changed, as well. Some of these changes are visible in these photos of a 1977 F-15A (green bay) and 1986 F-15C (white bay).

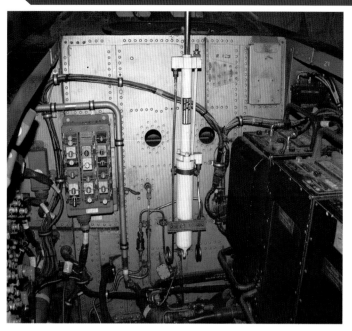

The canopy actuator is in the center of the rear wall. To the left of it is a relay panel, shown in detail below. To the right of the canopy actuator is a relay box. Further to the right, with a coiled line and yellow streamer attached, is the canopy actuator initiator as discussed on page 17. These are both removed on the green-bay F-15A at right, but normally present on the F-15A and F-15C. The cockpit pressure regulator lives inside the small hole above and aft of Bay 5, bottom right.

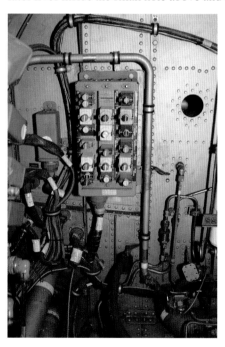

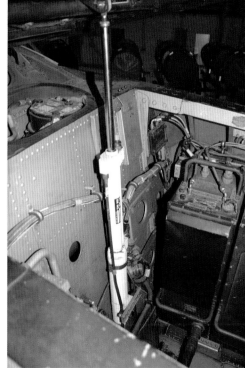

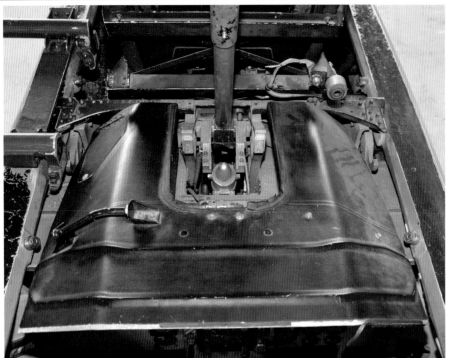

Similar to the front cockpit, a glareshield covers the rear instrument panel in the F-15B/D. It is identical in both models. The glareshield serves to protect the mass of cables and the backs of the instruments that live in this area. The canopy remover, top right, works in an identical manner to that found on the F-15A/C. Air is pumped into the canopy seal by the small fitting on the rear of the right side of the front ejection seat, left. A fitting is present on the canopy frame that connects to this to inflate the rubber canopy seal to pressurize the cockpit. A handhold, right, is found on the left side of the glareshield.

Greg Fieser

The rear cockpit of the two-seat F-15B/D is almost a mirror image of the front cockpit, only far less crowded. The rear cockpit features primitive flight/engine instrumentation, a smaller MCCP, and fire warning lights. The VSD, too, is present, although the rubber boot surrounding the front cockpit VSD is not. The F-15D cockpit is identical to the F-15B. Later jets, however, have additional NVIS (Night VISion) wiring present surrounding the MCCP at the top of the panel. This is not found on early aircraft. Unlike the front cockpit, the rear control stick has remained unchanged since delivery from the factory.

Greg Fieser

Greg Fieser

A circuit breaker panel is the most prominent object on the left sidewall in the rear cockpit. Cockpit lighting is also present on the sidewall. The rear cockpit's side panels are very sparse, with only a handful of controls present. The rear cockpit retains full flying controls, however, equipped with throttles, rudder pedals, and a control stick. The F-15B and F-15D rear cockpit is virtually identical to one another.

The Ejection Mode lever is at the lower right corner of the main instrument panel. Using this lever, the crew can choose the sequence in which each seat is ejected from the jet, and which has priority. It is the yellow/black striped lever below left.

The Instructor Pilot, VIP, or photographer in the back seat has his own oxygen controls. These are the red, white, and green levers at the forward edge of the panel, below. The oxygen/microphone tubing, right, is identical to that found in the front cockpit. With the exception of an added circuit breaker panel on the sidewall, above, the F-15D panel is nearly identical to the F-15B, which is shown at the top left of this page.

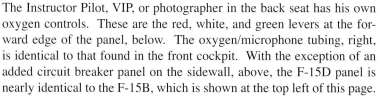

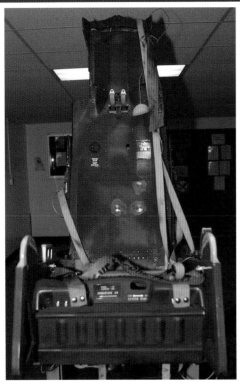

The F-15 uses the ACES II ejection seat, as does the A-10, F-16, F-22, F-117, B-1, and B-2. Ejection is enabled via a pair of yellow ejection handles located adjacent to the pilot's knees. A pair of environmental sensors are on either side of the headrest. These sense airspeed and altitude as the seat slides up the rails during ejection, then relay this information to the seat's recovery sequencer. This, in turn, uses this information to select the best recovery mode for ejection. Canopy breakers are installed

on the top of the seat to break through the canopy should the canopy fail to jettison automatically during the ejection sequence. On the lower portion of the seat, behind the two yellow ejection handles, are additional levers/handles. On the right side, shown at left, is the Emergency Manual Chute handle. This handle fires the main chute mortar to initiate seat separation in case of failure of the electronic sequencer. On the left side of the seat, the Safety Lever is immediately aft of the left ejection handle. When this lever is up/forward, the seat can not be ejected. The seat is armed via pulling the lever down/aft. This is done as the pilot taxies onto the runway for departure. The

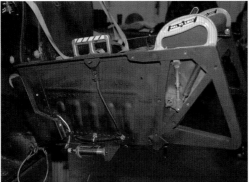

pilot's survival pack, below, is stowed under the seat pan. The pilot's harness buckles directly to the survival pack. During ejection, the pack separates from the seat automatically, and remains attached to the pilot. The majority of jets now have the black sheepskin cushions, replacing the original sage green cushions installed on early aircraft. The seat depicted on this page has obviously been removed from the aircraft for maintenance. It has had its parachute pack, normally mounted behind the headrest, removed. It is also lacking the bright green emergency oxygen bottle and seat cushions.

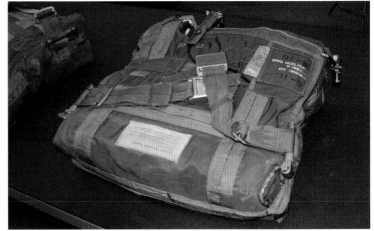

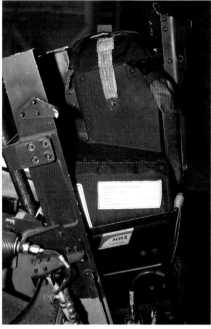

The canopy is designed to jettison from the aircraft during the ejection sequence before the seat begins to leave the aircraft. However, should there be a problem with this process, the seat is equipped with a pair of canopy breakers on the headrest in front of the pitots. These are sturdy enough to shatter the canopy to allow the seat/pilot through to safely escape the jet. At right, the seat rocket is visible on the bottom of the jet as the seat is removed for maintenance.

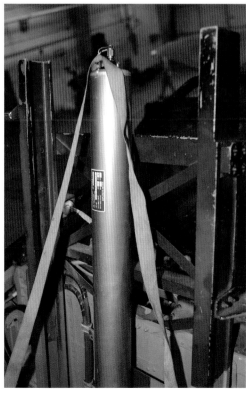

A closer look at the upper part of the seat reveals the two parachute risers that connect to the pilot's harness, at left. The two speed-sensing pitots are normally covered whenever the jet is parked and secured on the ground. The parachute is visible on the top of the seat. A current inspection placard is placed on the side of the seat, as well as placed into the pouch on the left side of the seat. The canopy breakers are also shown to good effect on this page.

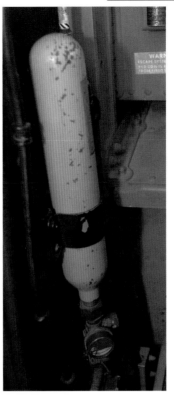

The green bottle on the side of the seat is the pilot's emergency oxygen supply in the event of a high altitude ejection. During the ejection sequence, the bottle fires automatically and allows the pilot to breathe through his mask normally until a lower altitude is reached. Should the bottle fail to fire automatically, the pilot can pull the green 'O' ring on the left side of the seat to activate the bottle manually. Below, this overall view of the bottom of the seat allows perfect viewing of the two ejection handles, the Emergency Manual Chute handle on the right side, and the arm/safe lever, black inertia reel release and emergency "O" ring activation handle on the left side. Also visible are the lap and survival kit belts.

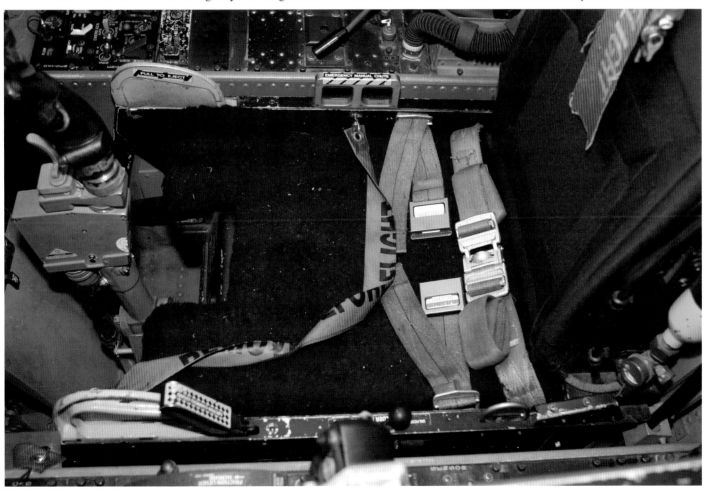

For all the similarities of the Strike Eagle to other Eagle versions on the outside, the inside of the cockpit is vastly different. Starting at the very front, a different glareshield over the front instrument panel is installed. Likewise, a new wide-angle HUD, along with new combining glass, is in place to allow the F-15E pilot to view imagery from the LANTIRN navigation pod. The front instrument panel itself is re-designed, giving the Strike Eagle a much more modern look and feel. The most obvious difference to the cockpit is the addition of three Multi-Purpose Display (MPD) screens. The center MPD screen is a 5" full-color screen (making it a Multi-Purpose Color Display, or MPCD), while the remaining two are 6" wide, but display only mono-chromatic green.

The F-15E introduced the Up-Front Controller (UFC) that replaced the MCCP on other Eagle versions. The UFC features a large keypad with six CRT (Cathode Ray Tube) text lines for digital data display and entry. This serves as the main avionics control point. All data is manually input into the navigation system and central computer using the UFC. An additional UFC is located in the rear cockpit for the WSO to use. The front and rear UFC can communicate with each other, allowing either the pilot or WSO to enter information into the jet's avionics/computers using either UFC. The last few F-15Es produced have a slightly different UFC, featuring LCD (Liquid Crystal Display) screens instead of the CRT screens featured on earlier jets (and shown on this page). Many of the export versions of the F-15E have the LCD panels, as well, including the F-15K and F-15S. The HUD control panel is mounted directly beneath the UFC, and works in a similar fashion as other Eagle models. However, it, too, is improved by the addition of the HUD mode switches directly onto the HUD control panel. Everything about the HUD can now be adjusted from one location. It also has a BIT function to check correct operation prior to flight.

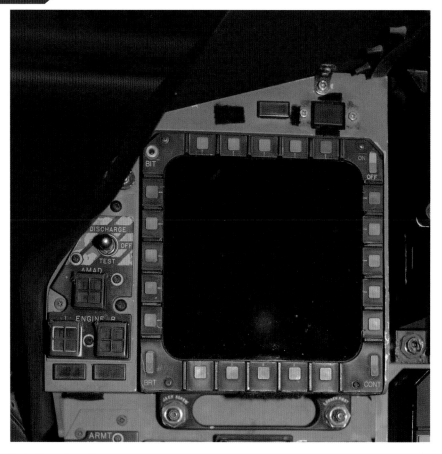

Each MPD can display up to nearly thirty screens, making the cockpit customizable for each pilot on each mission, or even mission segment. A collar

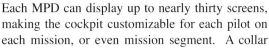

around the outside of each MPD holds 20 pushbuttons that allow the pilot to select his preference. The MPDs and HUD are the primary source of flight information; however, should either of these fail, or should the pilot prefer, traditional flight instruments are provided below the left MPD. The lower left corner of the instrument panel is similar to that found on other Eagle versions. The tailhook lever, landing gear handle/status lights, Emergency Gear Extension handle, and Pitch Ratio Indicator and control switch are all identical to the F-15A-D. Likewise, the F-15E is equipped with the same yellow/black-striped canopy jettison lever, below.

Although the fire warning panel is different (located to the left of the left MPD, above), its function remains the same as other models. On the center pedestal, below the center MPCD, the air-conditioning vent is still present, as are the circuit breaker panels that straddle it. The rudder adjustment knob is relocated slightly further down on the pedestal, to the right of the yellow Emergency Brake/Steer handle.

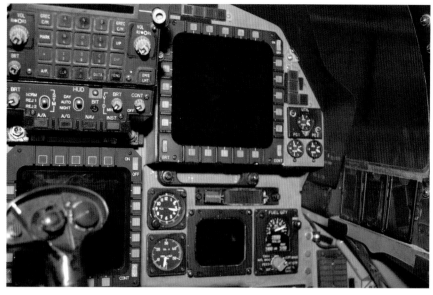

Many of the engine instruments have also been integrated into the MPDs, leaving only a few as traditional round gauges. The hydraulic instruments are to the right of the right MPD. Below that is the clock, fuel control panel, and pressure altitude gauge. The additional screen is the Engine Monitor Display, replacing several of the conventional round engine instruments. The center MPCD is visible behind the control stick. Although it is smaller than the two MPDs, it has the advantage of being able to display color. It has the ability to display a color moving map, with the aircraft's position superimposed over it, with a range of selectable scales, all the way down to 1:50,000.

The lower right corner of the front panel includes the JFS start handle, caution/warning light panel, and Emergency Vent handle, all similar to those found in other versions. The windscreen bow is a convenient place to stow abbreviated checklists, radio frequency lists, etc, as this F-15E shows below.

The F-15E's left side panel is similar in layout to the earlier Eagle versions. Panels for the fuel management, external aircraft lighting panel, autopilot control, ILS/TACAN, IFF, and radar control are again in place on the left panel. The BIT panel and Emergency air refueling slipway control are carried over from the F-15C cockpit. The guarded red switch at the front of the panel, below the landing gear handle is the Nuclear Consent switch.

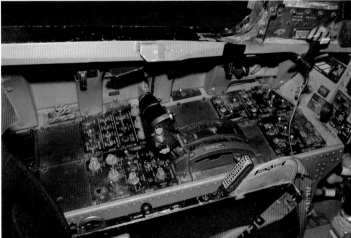

Above-- Visible on the side of the ejection seat is the left ejection handle and seat Safety Lever, shown in the "safe" position. With the lever in this position, ejection is disabled to prevent inadvertent ejection. The pilot arms the seat as he takes the runway for departure. In the armed position, the lever is rotated back and lays flat on top of the seat. When the pilot exits the runway after landing, he returns the lever up to its safe position. The emergency oxygen activation O'ring is aft of the safety lever.

The pilot connects his G-suit to the adaptor fitting at the rear of the left instrument panel, shown at right. The G-suit receives treated bleed air from the engines (treated in the Heat Exchanger) to inflate the G-suit during maneuvering flight. The inflating action squeezes the pilot's abdomen and upper and lower legs to force the blood from pooling in this area. This, in turn, forces more blood higher into the pilot's body, keeping oxygen flow to the brain. On average, the G-suit provides about one full extra G of tolerance for the pilot.

The F-15E's throttle quadrant is in an identical location to the F-15A-D models. It is very similar to the earlier jets, designed to fit into the hand of the pilot so that either throttle can be manipulated simultaneously. Movement of throttles works in the same fashion as other models, too. To increase thrust, the pilot moves the throttles forward. The throttles are in Idle Cut-off at the rear position, as shown in the photos. The throttles are again designed around the HOTAS concept. A total of nine buttons are on the throttles (three on the left, six on the right) that allow control of various controls. The speedbrake switch, microphone switch, and several weapons/radar controls are on the throttles, each designed to keep the pilot's hands on the throttles during crucial moments of flight. The silver switch outboard and aft on the throttle quadrant is the rudder trim switch. The photos below and below right nicely illustrate the location of the G-suit adaptor and the front cockpit bulkhead.

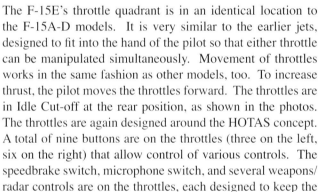

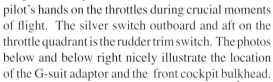

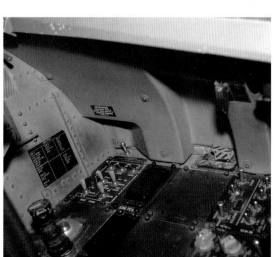

Jake Melampy

The F-15E sidewalls are identical to other versions. The canopy control handle is shown in detail at right, along with its hydraulic supply line. A cockpit flood light is built into the sidewall forward of the canopy control handle. The right side instrument panel retains many of the features found on the F-15A-D. The oxygen control panel remains at the front, along with the cockpit lighting control panel, anti-ice, generator, and heating/cooling controls. The F-15E adds AVTR control to the right side, something not found on earlier Eagles. The panel looks sparse compared to the "Light Greys." Noticeably absent from the side panel is the navigation keypad, which is integrated into the F-15E's UFC. Also missing is the ICMS and TEWS control panel, which is moved into the rear cockpit.

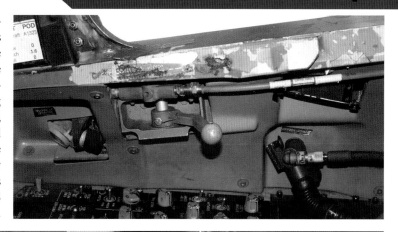

The remainder of the panel is identical, featuring the same oxygen, emergency oxygen, and microphone hoses sprouting from the rear of the panel. When not in use, the hose assembly can be clipped onto a stowage hook on the sidewall. Behind that is a map case, which in this instance has a custom panel courtesy of the jet's crewchief. The same maplight is present, as well. Its alligator clips allow it to be positioned nearly anywhere.

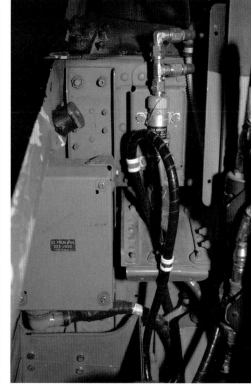

Like the throttle quadrant, the F-15E's control sticks are full of buttons for various functions. The pilot's stick, above, hosts seven buttons. On the top of the stick, from left to right, are the red weapons release button, "castle" multi-function switch, and aircraft trim switch. On the left side of the stick, designed for the pilot's thumb, is the Auto-Acquisition switch. Below that is the nose-wheel steering button. A traditional trigger is located at the front of the stick to fire the gun and start video. At the base of the stick grip, the lever that sticks up is the paddle switch. Each of these buttons has at least one purpose; many have several depending on the flight environment and mode set into the weapons computers. The WSO (Weapons Systems Officer) control stick, right, has several buttons, but not nearly as many. He has limited ability to do much more than fly the aircraft. The large grey box on the control stick below the grip is the stick sensor box. This box senses control stick pressure exerted by the pilot (or WSO). This pressure is converted into a signal that is fed to the aircraft's AFCS (Automated Flight Control System). The AFCS works in conjunction with a traditional mechanical flight control system to move the air-craft's flight controls. If either system fails, the other can handle the job alone.

The rear instrument panel is covered by a rigid plastic glareshield to protect the wire bundles and instruments. A handle is located on the top of the glareshield for use by the WSO (Weapons Systems Officer). The canopy locking mechanism and canopy remover are identical to that found on the F-15B/D, located immediately behind the front ejection seat (which is removed in the photo at right), in an indentation in the glareshield. Also in this area is the ECS ducting that mates with a fitting on the canopy rail for cockpit cooling. It is the black box next to the canopy remover. The canopy seal pressurization outlet is visible mounted to the rear of the right seat rail.

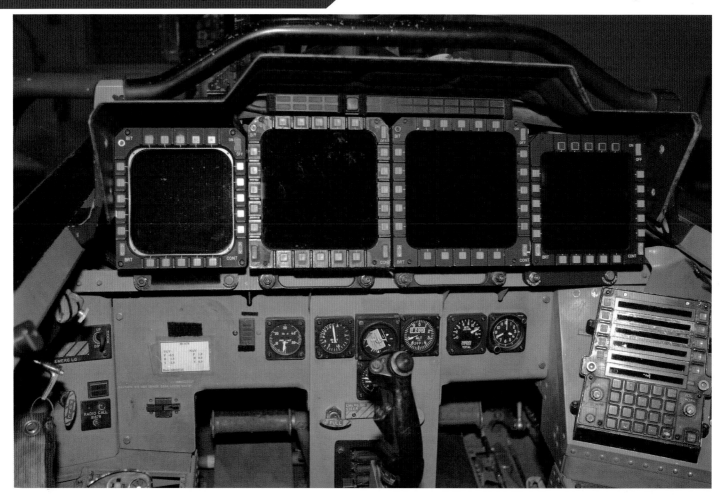

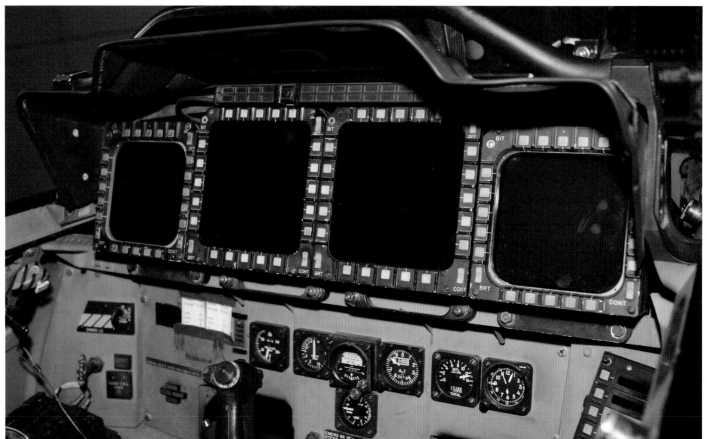

The WSO is treated to a pair of 6" MPDs in the center of the instrument panel, flanked by a pair of 5" MPCDs outboard. The screens are identical to those found in the front cockpit, customizable to each unique pilot's preferences and/or each phase of flight. The two center screens display only monochromatic green. However, the two outer screens display in full color. Above the MPD screens is the caution/warning light panel, above.

The MPD/MPCD can be selected to display basic flight information. However, traditional flight instruments are provided as a back-up to the digital screens, left. Cabin pressure is at the far left, followed by the airspeed indicator, Attitude Director Indicator (ADI), altimeter, fuel quantity, and clock. Below the ADI is the Vertical Velocity Indicator (VVI). The rudder pedal adjustment knob and Emergency Brake/Steer handle are carried over from the front cockpit and serve the same purpose. A cabin pressurization/heating/cooling outlet is below these. The WSO has his own UFC, below left, on the lower right panel for his use. This is nearly identical to the UFC found in the front cockpit. It lacks the HUD control panel, but otherwise functions in the same manner. This communicates with the front cockpit's UFC to share information. Either the pilot or WSO can enter information into the jet's computers using either UFC. To the right of this is the Ejection Mode selector handle. This is a three-position handle: Norm, Solo, and Aft Initiate. This lever can be used to select the best ejection sequence for the occasion. With the switch in Norm (the 12 O'clock position), activation of the rear seat ejection handle results in only the rear seat's ejection. Activation of the front seat's ejection handle after the rear seat's ejection results in only the forward seat's ejection. Activation of front cockpit's handle before rear cockpit's results in both seats leaving the jet. With the handle in the Solo position (10 O'clock position), activation of either seat's ejection handle results in both

Both aft cockpit sidewalls feature circuit breaker panels for various electrical systems. The left sidewall, above, retains the yellow/black-striped Emergency Canopy Jettison handle. It is secured by a pin when the jet is on the ground. A seat adjustment toggle switch is visible on the sidewall just forward of the throttle quadrant to raise or lower the ejection seat to suit the WSO's comfort. Above and forward of this is a cockpit floodlight built into the sidewall. Below, the lower corner of the WSO's main instrument panel is shown. The Emergency Gear Extension handle and hook lever are identical to those found in the front cockpit.

The WSO retains full flying capabilities in the rear cockpit, with retention of the flight control stick and throttle quadrant. Notice, however, the difference in the amount of buttons on the WSO's throttles. Only two buttons are present on the right throttle (speedbrake and microphone switches). The WSO has an additional pair of controls, however, not found in the front cockpit. One control is found on each side panel, above right. These are used to control the F-15E's sensor and weapons systems. Some of the controls found in the front cockpit are relocated to the rear in the F-15E. The ICMS and TEWS gear are among these items, located outboard of the throttle quadrant on the left side panel. The black box forward of the throttle quadrant is the 8mm AVTR tape deck. It is a relatively recent addition to the WSO's panel (added beginning in 1995) and not found on earlier jets. HUD footage and MPD/MPCD footage can be recorded for later use. Behind the throttle quadrant is a map case for stowage of various items, left. It is covered by a piece of fabric. The G-suit adaptor fitting is in the same location as found in the front cockpit.

The WSO's right sidewall also features the circuit breaker panel and cockpit floodlight similar to the left sidewall. The canopy control handle is also here. The right instrument panel is very small compared to the front cockpit's, but similar in function. Oxygen controls, heating/cooling, interior cockpit lighting, CMD (Counter Measure Dispense, or chaff/flare), and TEWS are all managed from the right panel. A control stick is present on the forward section of the panel for the WSO's use. It's functions are described on the next page. Visible on the seat below is the right ejection handle and manual chute release handle. Notice the Remove Before Flight streamer pinned to the latter.

The two side control sticks in the WSO's cockpit are his primary controls for doing his job. The WSO spends a large amount of time with his hands on these sticks. For comfort, wrist guards are built into the bottom of each stick, something not found on the flight control sticks on any Eagle model. For the most part, the sticks are identical to, and are a mirror copy of, each other. On the top of the sticks, each of the two outboard buttons are multi-functional. Each can be pushed down or "steered" up/down/left/right to choose a specific command. The result of each movement depends on which mode the MPD/MPCDs are in, which weapons are configured, etc. The most ouboard button is known as the "coolie" switch after its shape. It is used to input or select information displayed on the MPD/MPCD. The coolie switch on the left stick controls the left two MPD/MPCDs; the right coolie switch does the same for the right two screens. Outboard of these three buttons, on the side of each stick is another button. On the right stick, this is the IFF Interrogate switch. On the left stick, however, this is the CMD dispense switch to release chaff or flare. The remaining buttons on the stick are all multi-function switches. Their purposes are again dependant on which mode is selected in the MPD/MPCD.

The oxygen hose is identical to that in other Eagles, as is the maplight. Notice the difference in size of the circuit breaker panel vs. the panel found in the aft cockpit of the F-15D. This is a direct result of the additional avionics installed in the Strike Eagle for its mission. The aft bulkhead of the WSO cockpit differs from the front in the fact that it is covered by a quilted and padded fabric.

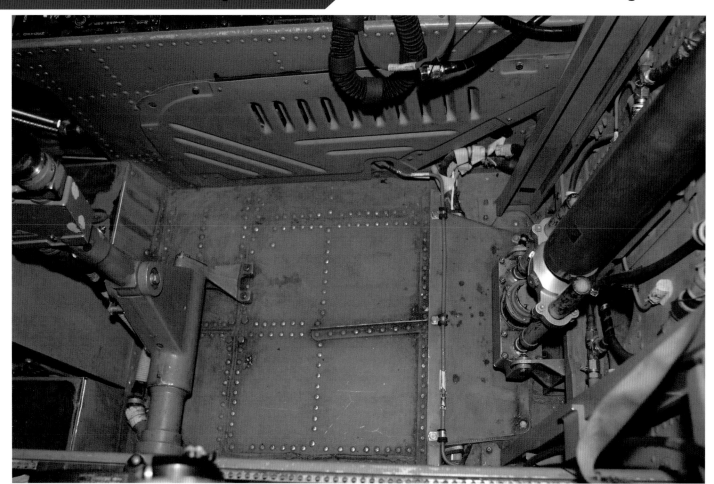

Jake Melampy

F-15E Rear Cockpit

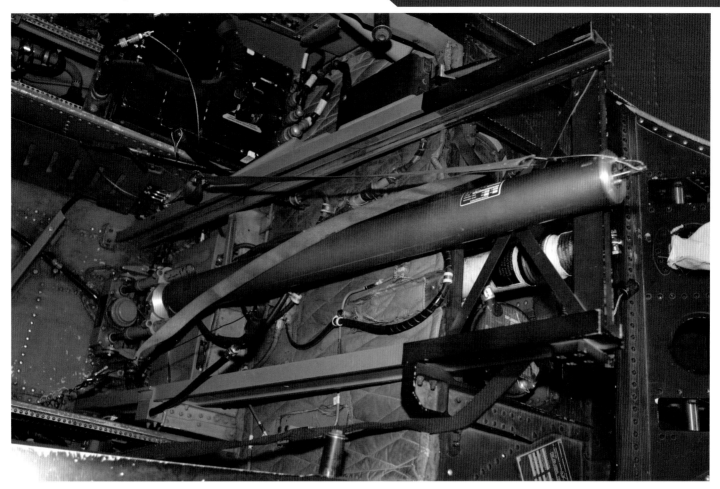

During maintenance, removal of the canopy, ejection seats, and most of the side panels gives a rare view into the cockpit. The bronze tube is the seat's rocket blast tube. It is ejected out of the jet along with the seat. The seat slides up the rails, which remain in the jet, during ejection. On the previous page, the top photo is the front cockpit floor.

The canopy actuator, right, is situated in a recess behind the rear cockpit (as it is in the F-15B/D models, as well). To its left, is the cockpit pressure regulator. Also visible against the bulkhead behind the canopy actuator is the canopy actuator intiator and its coiled lanyard that connects to the canopy. Its function is described on page 17.

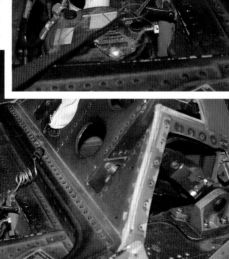

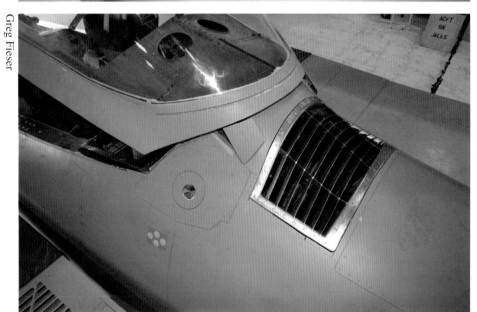

Greg Fieser

The large vent behind the canopy, left, is the Secondary Heat Exchanger Exhaust. It has a slightly different shape on the two-seat jets, below left. The Heat Exchanger on the Eagle is responsible for providing cool air to the avionics, as well as air for windscreen rain removal, cockpit pressurization, cooling, and G-suit inflation. Bleed air from the 13th stage engine compressor is routed to the Primary Heat Exchanger where it is initially cooled by mixing it with outside ram air (vents on the fuselage sides or CFTs, page 110 for the F-15A-D and 92 for the F-15E). This is called pre-conditioned bleed air. Next, the air is sent forward to the Secondary Heat Exchanger where it meets an ECS (Environmental Control System) turbine for further cooling. Finally, it then goes through a water separator to extract moisture before being sent forward for avionics cooling and cockpit air conditioning.

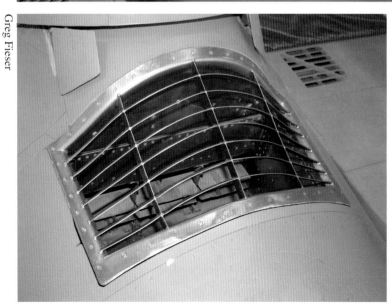

Greg Fieser

The round exhaust below and aft of the canopy on the jet's right side, below, is the Regenerative Heat Exchanger exhaust, used for ECS cooling. It was factory-installed on all Eagles up to F-15E 96-0200. These later F-15E's have had ECS package modifications to install a high-pressure water separator. With this mod, it was determined that the Regenerative Heat Exchanger was not needed, so it, along with its louvered exhaust outlet, was removed from all later Eagles. This modification can also be found on some F-15C/Ds. For the modelers, be sure to check your references!

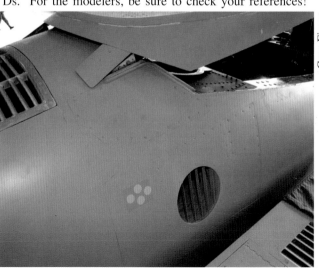

Greg Fieser

Above-- Immediately behind the heat exchanger exhaust is the round upper TA-CAN (TACtical Air Navigation) antenna. Behind it is the upper UHF blade antenna.

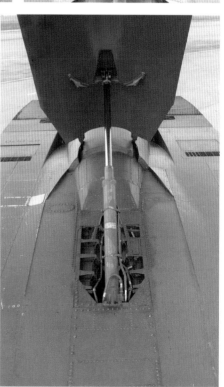

A speedbrake is located on top of the fuselage behind the canopy. It increases drag drastically to slow the aircraft down quickly. It is raised and lowered by a large hydraulically-powered actuating strut. The F-15 speed brake requires hydraulic power to open. With the jet shut down the speed brake simply lays on top of the jet, and can be lifted up by hand. If maintenance is required with the engines not running, a red metal collar, above, is fitted around the actuating strut to keep the speed brake open. The F-15E speedbrake is shown. Other models' speedbrakes are similar; however only the F-15E has the built-in hand-hold at the rear trailing edge of the speedbrake.

The air induction system in the engine intakes work hand in hand with the aircraft's computers to achieve the optimum airflow into the engines for peak performance. Each air intake system slows the air entering the intake, which compresses the air flowing into the engine. Four ramps (First, Second, Third, and Diffuser) vary the amount of air entering each intake to achieve the amount of compression of that air. Each of the doors are connected to each other, and work together for a seamless operation largely unnoticed by the pilot. Each ramp (with the exception of the Diffuser ramp) has perforations on the surface to improve the efficiency of the intake.

These tiny holes allow excess air to bleed away into the airstream outside of the intake through louvers that are placed in various places along the outside of the intake. Exit louvers are placed on each side and top of the First ramp and aft of the bypass door.

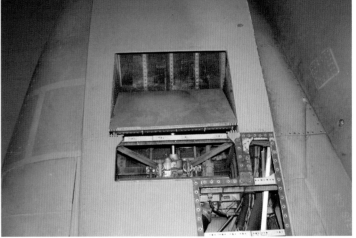

Bypass doors, above and right, are in place to provide the air induction system the ability to lower the speed and pressure of the air inside the intake by venting some of the air overboard. The door opens and closes to adjust the speed of the air flow through the intake and lower the pressure inside. The door is hinged to the airframe and opens towards the front. The bypass door actuator is visible in the photo above. The door itself is pictured in the fully open position.

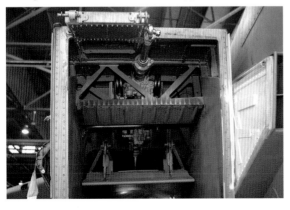

With the inlet removed from the jet, a better view of the ramp actuators is possible (far left). Also visible is the inlet hinge point at the bottom of the intake opening (left).

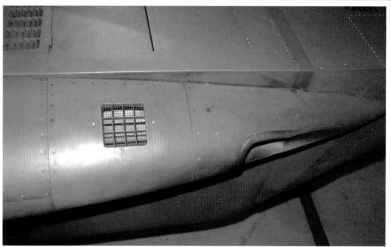

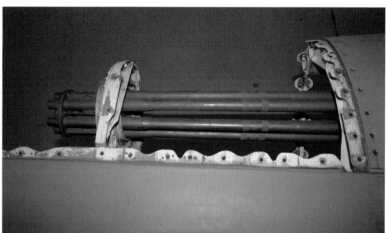

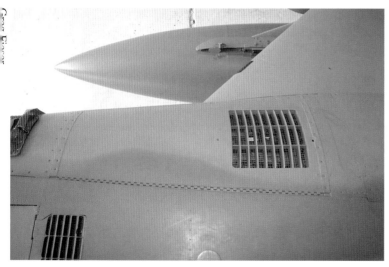

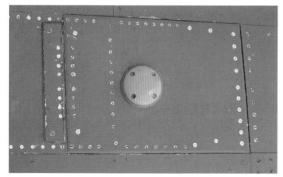

The M61A1 20mm cannon is mounted on the jet's right side, outboard of the right engine intake. Vents allow gun gasses to escape away from the engine intake. At left, a GPS antenna is placed along the top of the fuselage, next to the speed-brake. Its general location is shown in the photo top left of this page. The GPS is part of the EGI (Embedded GPS/INS) system installed in all F-15Es begining in 1996, and recently added to many late-build F-15C/Ds. The EGI is the Eagle's primary navigation instrument. The system is a combination of a GPS signal that gives constant updates to the Inertial Navigation System's ring-laser gyroscopes.

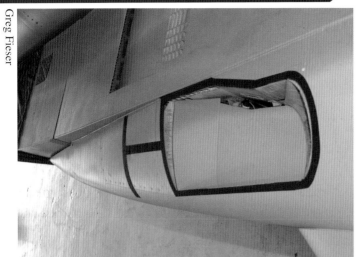

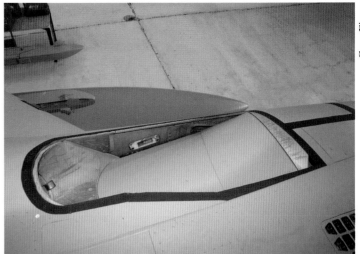

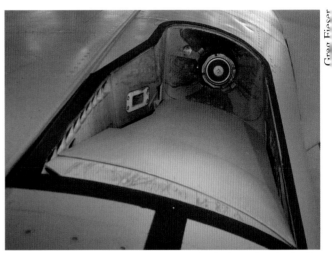

The aerial refueling receptacle is located adjacent to the left intake, forward of the wings. The ability to air-refuel gives the Eagle the obvious advantage of increased range and mission length, subject only to pilot endurance. Many of the missions during Operation Desert Storm lasted over 8 hours, and even longer missions took place during Operation Enduring Freedom in 2001/2002. The slipway door consists of two doors that connect to one another by a linkage. The forward door hinges to the airframe at the leading edge. The rear door covers the receptacle that receives the tanker's boom. The door is powered by the Utility hydraulic system under normal circumstances. However, provisions are in place for the door to be opened in the event of hydraulic failure or normal system failure. The fuel system is depressurized when the slipway door is opened.

In this photo sequence, a 131st Fighter Wing F-15C of the Missouri ANG takes on fuel from a 126th Air Refueling Wing KC-135E over the skies of Missouri. The F-15 flies formation under and behind the tanker based on light signals from the bottom of the KC-135's fuselage. The "boomer" in the tanker than steers the boom into the Eagle's receptacle to begin the fuel transfer.

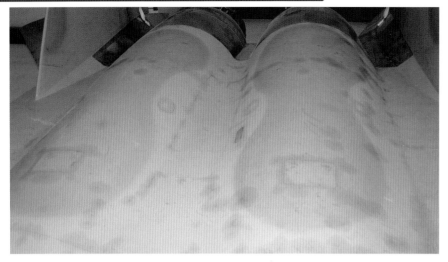

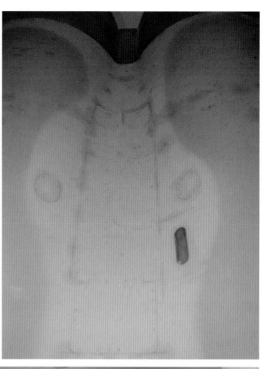

Aft of the speedbrake, the engine humps become much more pronounced. Noticeable on the forward part of each hump is a panel that provides access to the engine's forward mount. The oval screen between the engine humps is the JFS (Jet Fuel Starter) chimney. Notice that it is off-set to the left of the jet's centerline. The photo below left is looking towards the front of the jet. The photos above and above right are both looking towards the rear.

Greg Fieser

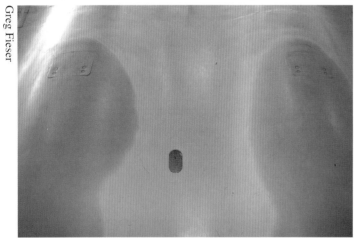

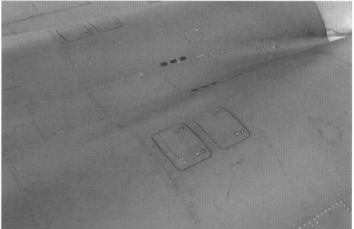

The F-15E, however, differs a bit from the "light greys". Pictured at left and above right, it has two access doors on each engine hump. In addition, it has six JFS chimney screens rather than the single screen found on the F-15A-D. Also visible in the photo below left is the aft end of the speedbrake and the fairing built into the fuselage. Additional avionics are stuffed into recesses between the engines, necessitating access panels which can be seen forward of the JFS screens.

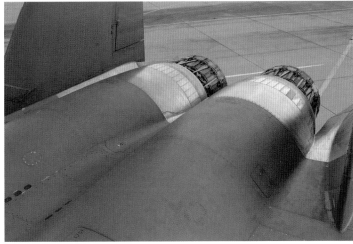

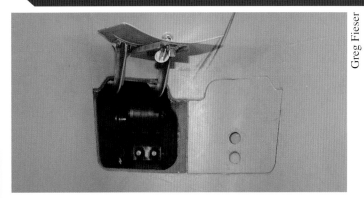

Greg Fieser

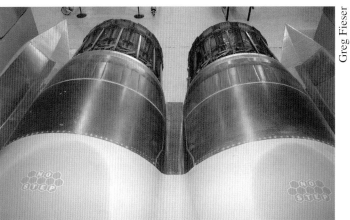

Greg Fieser

The aft engine mounts are accessed through a pair of doors located on the jet's centerline, aft of the JFS chimney screens. The area surrounding the engines is made of heat-resistant titanium. The color of this area can vary greatly depending on a number of factors, including age of the jet, number of flight hours, and atmospheric conditions. Notice that the titanium panels extend onto the base of the vertical stabilizers. Also notice the texture and pattern visible in the titanium plating.

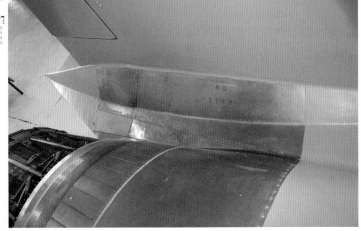

Greg Fieser

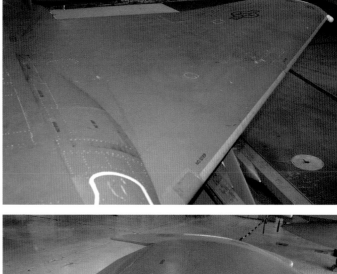

The Eagle's wing area is enormous, especially when compared to other fighters of its era (F-16, for example). The very low wing loading results in excellent turn performance. As a testiment to the strength of the wing, all models of the Eagle share the same wing construction/assembly, including the much higher-gross weight F-15E. A large portion of the F-15's internal fuel is stored inside the wings.

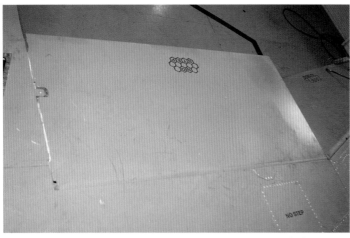

The F-15's flaps, left and below left, are inboard of the ailerons, above. The flaps are normally up on the ground, but lowered for all take-offs and landings. The ailerons, however, are usually lowered on the ground due to loss of hydraulic pressure. This allows them to sag towards the ground after flight.

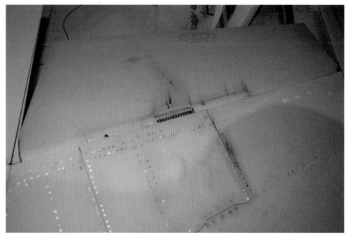

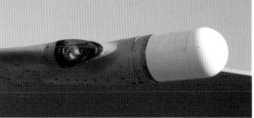

Like any aircraft, position lights are on both wingtips: red on the left, green (although the lens is decidedly blue-ish) on the right. The white domes are part of the AN/ALR-56 Radar Warning Receiver system.

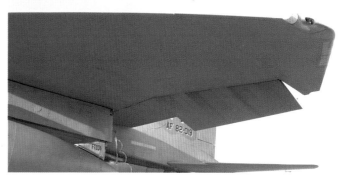

Above and above right-- The underside of the wings, again showing the normally-drooped aileron and the flaps in the up position. Notice the position of the RWR antenna and the position lights on the wingtips. The bottom of the aileron is again shown at right, while the bottom of the flap is below.

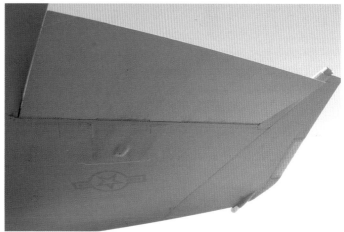

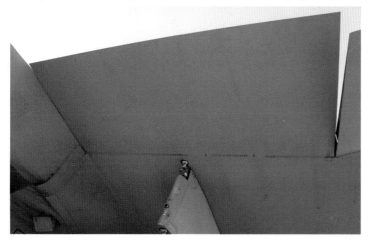

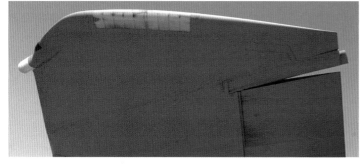

Besides the red/green position lights, formation strip lighting is on the wingtips, above. At the inboard leading edge of the wing is another pair of red position lights, right. The position lights of the F-15E, below, differ slightly from other versions. They are smaller and set further inboard than their counterparts on the "light grey" Eagles.

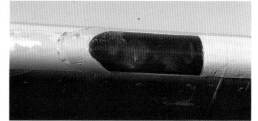

The forward part of the F-15's fuselage is little more than storage for the cockpit, nose landing gear, and avionics. Both sides of the jet feature large doors that open to allow access to the jet's avionics. The two doors immediately behind the radome open to reveal the radar's components, following page. The doors are secured closed by three quick-release fasteners along the door's bottom edge, below right.

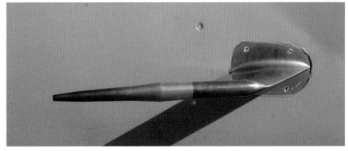

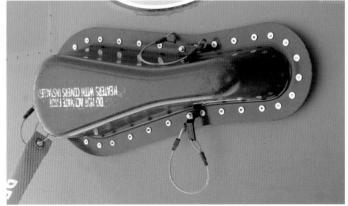

The rectangular antenna on the side of the door is the flush-mounted EWWS (Electronic Warning Warfare System) antenna. An additional EWWS antenna is located directly in front of the windscreen (page 13). Each door has a pitot tube, above right, mounted to it. The pitots are often covered by a protective cover, right, when the jet is parked on the ground to prevent damage.

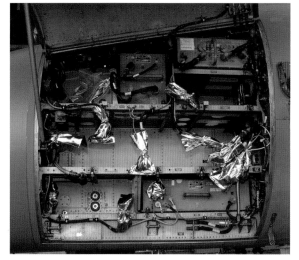

The avionics access bays (bay 3L, above and right; bay 3R, below and below right) is home to many of the radar's components. The bay above has had most of its components removed to reveal the empty shelves. It is important to point out that, while the basic layout of these bays remains constant from one jet to the next, many of the individual components are different, all depending on timeframe of individual modifications to the jets, and the type of Eagle (F-15A vs. F-15E, for example). A perfect example is the two photos of the the right bay, below and right. Both are F-15Cs, but each has a slightly different configuration. Both photos were taken on the same day.

The bay doors (door 3L, right, and door 3R, far right), hinge upward to reveal the equipment beneath. Both are secured by a proprod to hold them open. The wiring leading onto the inside of the door is for the pitot tube and EWWS antenna.

Two additional avionics and electrical component storage bays are located on each side of the fuselage beneath the cockpit. The left side of the fuselage is shown on this page. An Angle Of Attack (AOA) probe, above right, is located under the windscreen and above the forward avionics bay. Similar to the pitot tubes, the AOA probe is often treated to a protective cover when the jet is parked and secured.

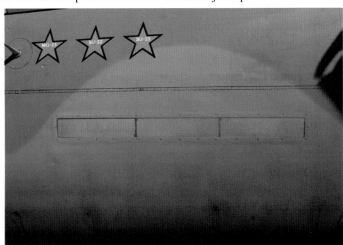

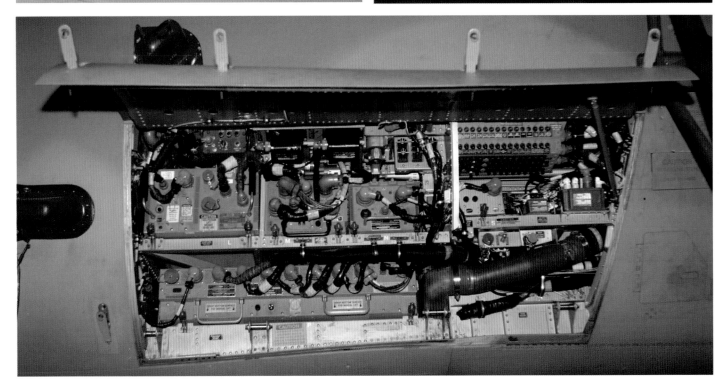

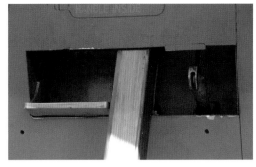

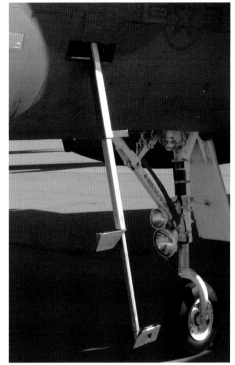

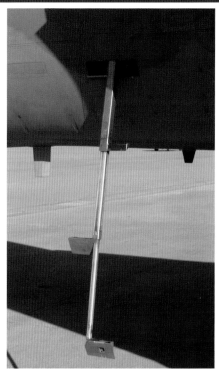

Above, right, and far right-- A telescoping boarding ladder is installed between the two avionics bays along the left side of the fuselage. It is extended by releasing a spring-loaded latch, and stowed simply by pushing the ladder up into the fuselage until it latches into place.

Below and below right-- To aid the pilot in his ascent to the cockpit, a recessed step and handle is built into the fuselage side along with the ladder. The handle, shown below, can be folded down when needed, while the step has a spring-loaded cover. The pilot's boot pushes the door open as he steps into the recess. At right, the handle is in the top left corner of the photo, while the recessed step is in the middle left of the photo, directly below the vertical black stripe. To the right of the step is the canopy control handle, used to raise and lower the canopy from outside the cockpit.

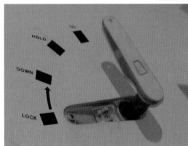

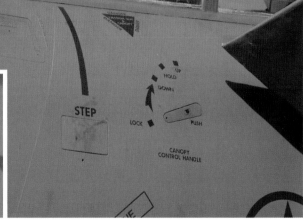

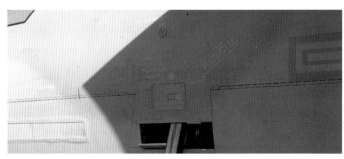

Left and above-- Above the ladder is the Emergency Canopy Jettison lever, hidden behind an access door. Above that, found only on the F-15A/C is the manual canopy unlock keyhole used to raise the canopy if/when there is insufficient pressure in the reservoir to open the canopy normally. The F-15B/D/E does not have this because of the additional weight of the two-seater's canopy. These models have a similar unlock mechanism in the nose landing gear well. On all Eagles, a 1/2" breaker bar is inserted into the keyhole to manually pump hydraulic pressure sufficiently to force the canopy actuator to move, thus raising the canopy.

Aft of the built-in crew boarding ladder is yet another access door for avionics and electrical components. Among other items, a transformer rectifier and the left Air Inlet Controller (AIC) is installed in this bay. The green tube with orange bands at the top of the bay is an ECS cooling line that supplies cooling air to the forward avionics bays and cockpit. As with the forward avionics doors, these doors can sometimes differ from one airframe to the next depending on version and serial number. These photos depict an F-15C.

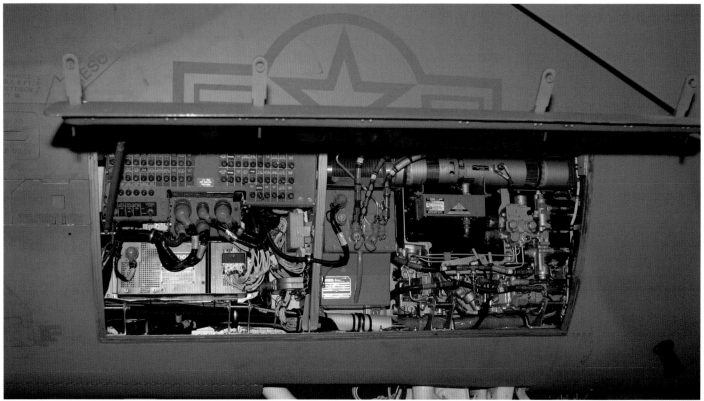

A TAT (Total Air Temperature) probe, right, is present aft and above the nose landing gear on both sides of the fuselage.. It supplies atmospheric information (air temperature/density) to the Air Data Computers. It is unpainted bare metal and electrically heated during flight to prevent ice formation. Immediately behind the nose landing gear door is the ICMS Band 1 antenna. At bottom right is the F-15E, which lacks an ICMS antenna here, while the photo above depicts an F-15C. The Secondary Heat Exchanger is in the bay behind the vent aft of the nose gear door.

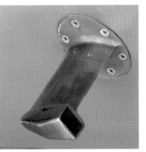

An additional AOA vane, above, is located on the right side of the fuselage, just aft of door 3R. Likewise, an additional formation strip light is present, as well. More avionics are located along the right side of the fuselage. The round green bottle is the Liquid Oxygen (LOX) tank that provides breathing oxygen for the pilot through his mask.

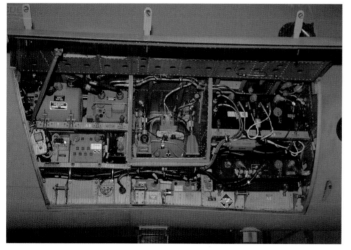

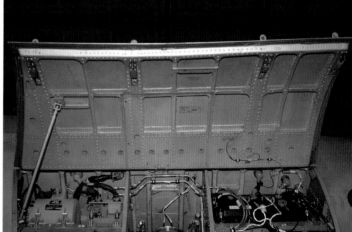

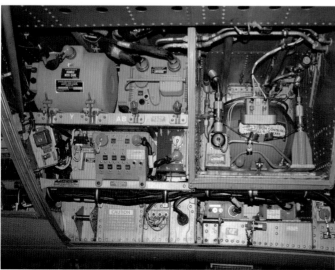

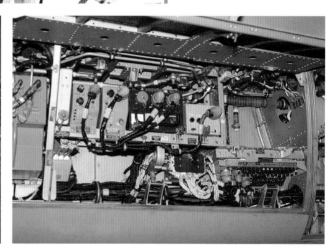

The jet's intakes for its two engines are located on either side of the fuselage, adjacent to the cockpit. To help control and regulate airflow into the engine, the forward part of each intake is hinged at the bottom, allowing it to open or close to allow more or less airflow into

the engine as needs dictate. Notice that on the ground with the engines not running, the intakes are always in their full open position (previous page top), but once an engine is started, the intake closes slightly (previous page bottom). In addition to this, the intakes' ramps are controlled by a computer called the Air Inlet Controller (AIC). However, on F-15E's, the AICs are being replaced by an Air Data Proccessor (ADP). During normal engine start, the first ramp (out of four) lowers to its full down position. Once in flight, the ramps are in constant and independent motion to ensure the correct volume of air is entering the intake. At .80 Mach, the first ramp raises and then the diffuser ramp (the last ramp just inside the intake) begins to lower to decrease the effects of the supersonic airflow entering the engine inlet.

Each intake is separated from the fuselage by the ACACS (Air Cycle Air Conditioning System) inlets, below and below right, also commonly referred to as the secondary heat exchanger. The ACACS cools air coming from the primary heat exchangers to be used for cockpit air-conditioning and to cool the jet's avionics.

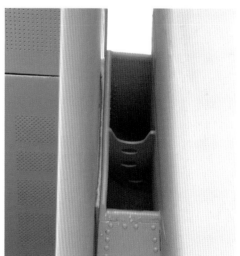

Many styles of intake covers are in use with the F-15, ranging from the hard plastic inserts, left, to the foam plugs, above and above right, to the full intake covers, right. They all have the same job however: to prevent foreign objects from entering the engines.

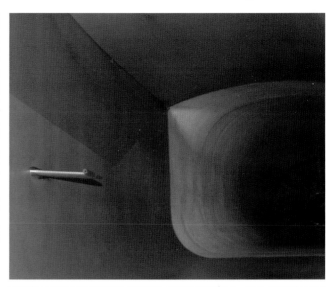

A look down the intake reveals the ducting leading to the engines buried deep within the fuselage. The jet's paint leads into the intake by several feet. The remainder of the intake ducting is off-white in color, and usually stained by scuff marks, etc. On the outboard wall of each intake is a probe, right, that provides air data to the Air Inlet Controllers.

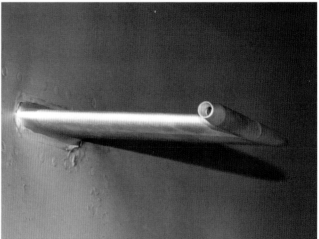

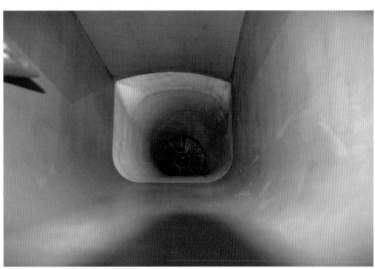

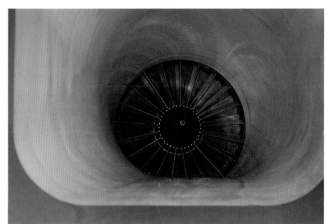

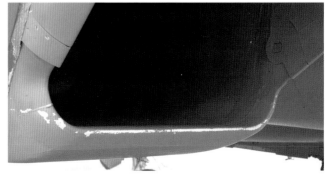

All versions of the Eagle share the same General Electric M61A1 20mm cannon. This weapon, with relatively minor differences, is the same gun found in the F-4E/F, F-16, F-18, and many other aircraft. The gun assembly is found in the jet's right wingroot, with the exception of the ammunition drum, which is mounted between the jet's intakes. The gun is electrically controlled, but driven by the jet's utility hydraulic system. As the gun is fired, the barrels rotate to allow effective cooling of the barrels, thus increasing gun/barrel life. The Strike Eagle's gun is slightly modifed when compared to the "light grey" Eagles'. To allow additional room for avionics, a linkless gun feed system was designed for the F-15E. Additionally, the capacity of the F-15E's ammunition drum was reduced to 450 rounds vs. the 940 rounds available to other versions. Externally, a large hump is present on the ammunition loading door of the F-15E, page 115. Access doors below the gun are located on the bottom of the wingroot, below left and below right. Notice the repair patches around the doors of a modern jet, below right, not found on the earlier jets, below left. These have been added around the airframe on high-use areas such as fasteners and latches as the jets have aged.

The two access doors on the bottom of the wingroot, also shown on the previous page, are opened up for a peek inside. The gun barrels are in the forward door (above left at the right of the photo), while the gun breech assembly is at the rear (above). Several panels are removed from the jet to remove the gun assembly from the jet, below. The gun is removed periodically depending on local conditions, ie. sandy or unusually rainy weather. More commonly, it receives a basic gun lube every 30 days, and inspected during the post-flight inspection at the end of each flying day. Regardless of use or local conditions, it is removed for inspection every 18 months.

The right side of the F-15A-D fuselage along the intakes is fairly plain, lacking access panels, etc. However, two built-in LAU-106 missile rails are located on each side of the jet. The LAU-106 was originally designed to load the AIM-7 Sparrow, but nowadays is most often fitted with the lighter AIM-120 AMRAAM. The right forward rail is numbered station 7, while the rear is station 6. The black-outlined access door aft of the blade is to direct fire extinguishing agent into the engine bays in the event of a fire on the ground.

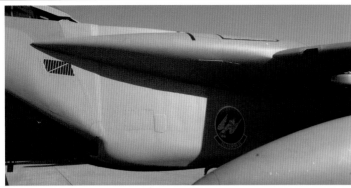

The left side of the F-15A-D is a mirror image of the jet's right side, with the exception of the absence of the gun in the wing-root. The same two LAU-106 launchers are present. The left missile launchers are numbered station 3 at the front, and station 4 at the rear. Each LAU-106 is gas powered. The missile is pushed away from the aircraft using explosive gases from cartridges screwed into sleeves adjacent to each launcher. Two types of sway braces have been used on the LAU-106. The type found in the large photo at the bottom of this page is designed for use with the AIM-7 Sparrow. The type with the insert, shown in the inset below right, is the newer type used with the AIM-120.

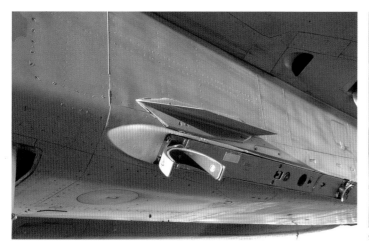

The aft LAU-106 is identical to the that on the front station. Each misile launcher has two ejector assemblies to push the missile away from the aircraft during launch. The forward ejector doubles as a swaybrace to help secure the missile to the jet's fuselage during flight. The blade above the launcher is a vortex generator which serves to stabilize the air around the launcher and its missile to help with separation of the missile from the jet during launch. It creates an extra downward push on the missile to further aid separation.

To increase the F-15E's fuel capacity, Conformal Fuel Tanks (CFTs) were added to the jet's fuselage beneath the wings. Each CFT bolsters the fuel capacity by an additional 750 US gallons. In addition, the tanks permit additional carriage of weapons. These are mounted to short integral pylons to further reduce drag and increase the F-15E's range. In addition, each CFT retains the LAU-106 missile launch rail found on the "light grey" F-15A-D. The CFT weapons stations are numbered beginning at the left rear of the longest CFT pylon at the bottom of the jet. This stations is known as station LCT-1. Station LCT-2 is the middle station, while LCT-3 is the forward station on the long CFT pylon. The stub pylons are numbered LCT-4, LCT-5, and LCT-6, again beginning at the rear and ending at the forward left stub pylon. The right CFT stations are numbered in an identical fashion, from RCT-1 through RCT-6. The LAU-106 stations are numbered the same as on the F-15A-D models. Station 3 is the left forward station, 4 is the left rear, 6 is right rear, and 7 is right front.

The CFTs are sometimes removed from the F-15E for maintenance and placed onto a custom stand. A single CFT can be removed from the jet in about thirty minutes. A rubber gasket runs the perimeter of each CFT, ensuring a tight seal against the aircraft to reduce drag. The CFT attaches to the Eagle via four large attachment points along the Strike Eagle's fuselage.

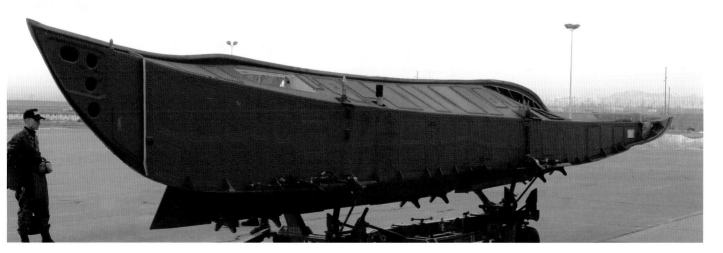

Zach Falzon

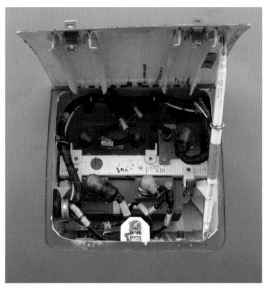

Zach Falzon

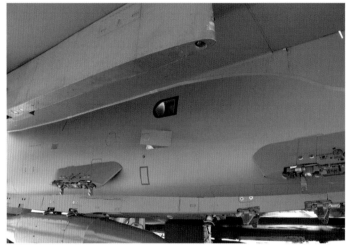

Right and below-- Fire extinguisher access is again marked by a black-outlined door, below. Below this is a spring-loaded inlet for the Primary Heat Exchanger. This door is on all Eagles with the Pratt & Whitney F100-PW-220 engines installed, including F-15A-D. It closes at .80 Mach, but remains open all other times. On F-15Es that are equipped with the more powerful F100-PW-229 engine (F-15E 90-0233 and subsequent), the spring-loaded door is replaced by a large fixed scoop, right, because these engines require a larger volume of air. They are often covered to prevent foreign object entry, below right.

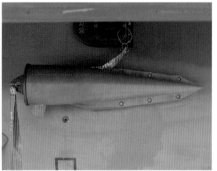

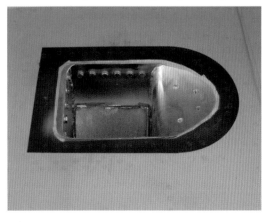

The Refuel Lockout Valve is a manual precheck valve that locks out the CFT during manual refueling. This allows the refuel pressure to bypass the precheck valve and refuel the CFT manually. This is most often performed during maintenance. Notice the rubber gasket that runs around the perimeter of the CFT. The access doors along the sides of the CFTs provide access to the CFT's attachment points to the jet, as well as storage for additional equipment, previous page, left.

The forward CFT pylon along the bottom of the CFT is known as LCT-3 on the left side, below left, and RCT-3 on the right side, above and below. All of the bottom CFT pylon stations are equipped with the BRU-47/A bomb release unit, compatible with the latest satellite-guided weapons.

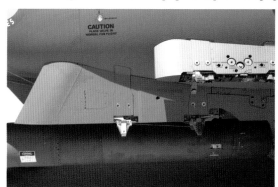

The Strike Eagle is equipped with the same LAU-106 missile rails as its "light grey" cousins. Two are mounted in each CFT pylon. The aft two launchers (shown next page) are always mounted towards the rear of the pylon. The location of the forward LAU-106 rails, however, varies depending on use. The majority of time, it is located between the two forward CFT stations, similar to the aft LAU-106. This is a storage facility, and the missile launcher cannot be used in this position. When the F-15E is in an air-air configuration, the forward LAU-106 is placed in the forward position normally occupied by LCT-3 and RCT-3. The BRU-47 bomb release units, then, are moved back into the storage facility normally occupied by the forward LAU-106. This allows the forward LAU-106 (stations 3 and 7) to function as an air-air weapons station, while rendering the BRU-47 non-functional. This configuration is shown at left and above right. At left is a South Korean F-15K, complete with a captive AIM-120A and IRST (InfraRed Search and Track) built into the LANTIRN pylon.

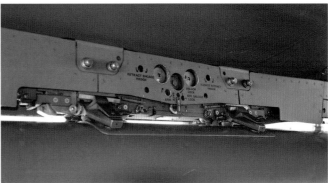

The middle two CFT pylon stations are LCT-2, seen above with a travel pod attached and right, and RCT-2, above right.

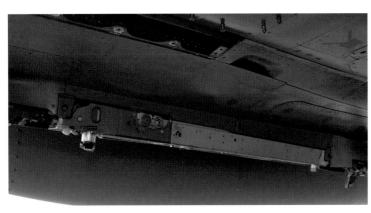

LCT-1 and RCT-1 are the aft pylons on the CFT. LCT-1 is on the left side of the jet, below, while RCT-1 is on the jet's right side, right and below right. Visible in both photos is the aft ejector piston of the rear LAU-106 missile launcher, shown above. The aft LAU-106 is located between the CFT stations (station 4 is between LCT-2 and LCT-1, for example). The rails are integrated into the CFT pylons.

Zach Falzon

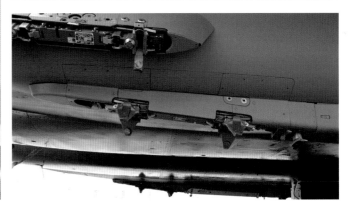

Jake Melampy

The outboard stub pylons on the CFT are each equipped with the BRU-46 bomb release unit. The forward stub pylons are LCT-4 and RCT-4. The early stub pylons had an angled leading edge, right. This angled piece was made of plastic and served only as an aerodynamic cover for the pylon to reduce drag. It was susceptible to cracking, and by 2004, largely replaced by a newer, more rigid, straight cover , below and below right. However, it is not impossible to find a jet still fitted with the angled piece.

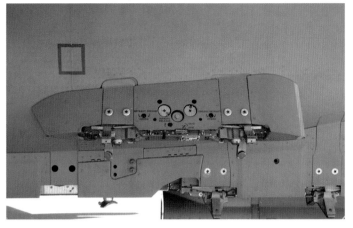

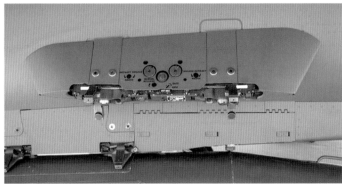

LCT-5, above, and RCT-5, right, are the middle stub pylons, while the aft stub pylons are LCT-6, below, and RCT-6, below right.

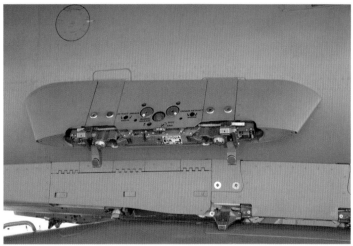

The F-15K has an extended aft fairing on each of the stub pylons on the CFTs. At left, LCT-6 is shown, looking at the rear of the pylon looking forward. Each of the remaining five pylons is similar.

A pair of vertical stabilizers rests atop the fuselage. Having two in place of the more standard single stabilizer improves stability and maneuverability. Although constructed of different materials, the stabilizer of the F-15E is visually identical to that found on the "light grey" Eagles.

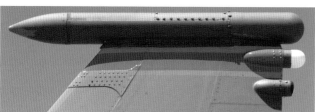

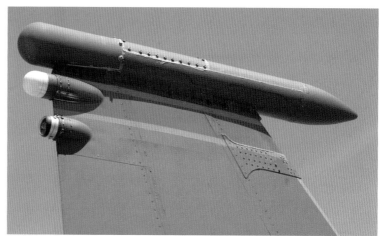

Above and above right-- An ALR-56 RWR (Radar Warning Receiver) antenna is positioned in the aft end of the "bullet" on the top of the left side stabilizer. To counter its weight, an aerodynamically-shaped ballast is placed on the top of the right side vertical stab, below and

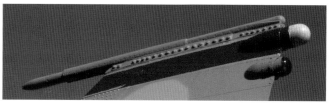

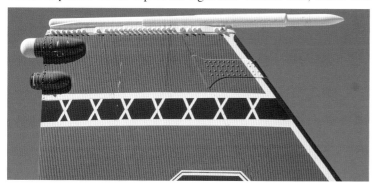

above. Both the RWR antenna and the ballast are identical for all Eagle models. Some foreign users of the Eagle, notably Japanese and Israeli jets, do not have the RWR antenna on the tail. In this instance, the small ballast is found on the top of each vertical stabilizer. Conversely, the Korean F-15K has the large antenna on both vertical stabs. A reinforcement plate was added to all Eagles in the mid-1980's to reinforce the torque box that supports the ECM bullet and ballast weight. This area was prone to cracks before the plate was added.

Above and above right-- A pair of AN/ALR-56 RWR antenna are mounted to the rear of the vertical stabilizers, one antenna on each stabilizer. Most are covered by a white fairing at the aft tip of the antenna. Below the RWR is an anti-collision light. On the left stabilizer, the light is white with a clear lens, while a red light is on the right stabilizer.

Below-- Hydraulically-actuated rudders are mounted to the rear of each stabilizer. In flight, the Eagle's rudders only move in the same direction, and in unison to each other. On the ground, however, the rudders can be moved by hand once the hydraulic pressure bleeds off. In this instance, it is not uncommon to see each rudder splayed in different directions, either after an inspection from ground crewmembers or from the wind's effects.

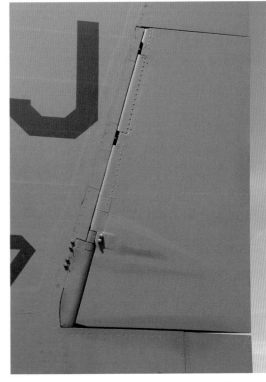

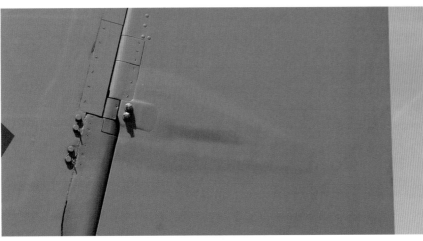

There have been many variations of rudders installed on F-15s over the years. Early rudders had no bulge at the base, but were strengthened after initial problems with the rotary actuator. The strengthening resulted in the distinctive bulge, left. The size of the bulge, too, has changed over the years. Many jets now have no bulge present at all, but signs of the reinforcement still remain.

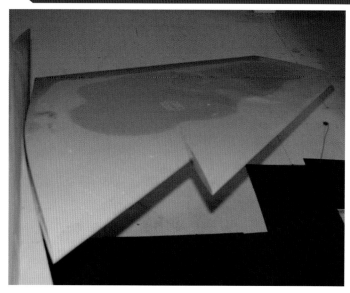

A pair of all-moving horizontal stabilators provides pitch control on the Eagle. All versions of the Eagle stabilators share the same basic construction. They move independantly of one another in flight. Once on the ground, they are prone to drooping in similar fashion to the ailerons.

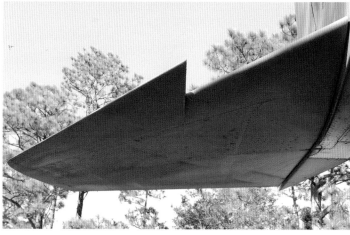
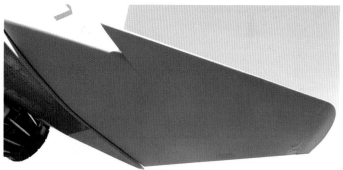
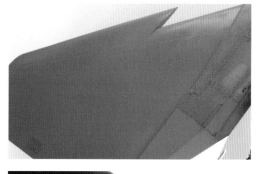
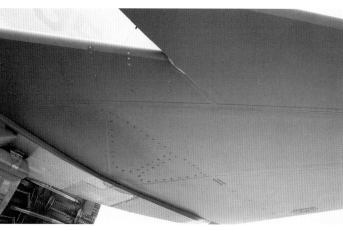

The F-15E's stabilators, above and right, differ slightly from other versions. These stabilators are constructed of a gridlock composite material instead of the honeycomb material used on earlier jets. They feature a visible sealant strip, running along the span behind the "dogtooth," installed over the seams of the gridlock panels, a detail not found on the other stabilator type. As the F-15 fleet ages, it is possible to find the newer, F-15E-style, stabilator on the F-15A-D models through attrition as those jets' stabilators are replaced.

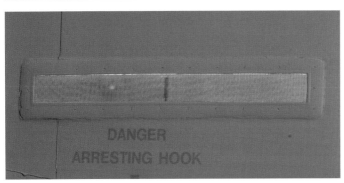

A pair of formation strip lights are mounted just aft of the wing. The South Korean F-15K differs from other variants in that its formation lights are NVG-compatible (shown next page). On the F-15E and post-MSIP F-15A-Ds (left side only on F-15A/B; right side only on F-15C/D), the formation light is broken into two separate parts. An access bay was added in this location on these jets, requiring the split of the lights. The F-15E's CFTs continue past this area, as shown in the pair of photos above and above left. Below, the Georgia state shape contains information on the jet's paintjob. Specifically, the date of application, paint colors, and location of paintwork are included. In this instance, this jet was painted at the F-15 depot at Warner Robins AFB, Georgia.

The F-15E's CFTs end underneath the horizontal stabilizers, above. Again, the rubber gasket that runs the perimeter of the CFT is plainly visible.

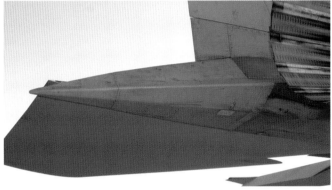

The tail booms aside of each engine have been modified over the years. The original F-15A/B booms, above, come to a sharp point at the rear tip. However, the MSIP F-15C/D boom was modified to include an aft-facing ALQ-135 ECM antenna on the right tailboom, below and below right. The F-15E has an additional antenna on its left tailboom, bottom. Three separate kinds of antenna are common on the F-15E, all of which are pictured.

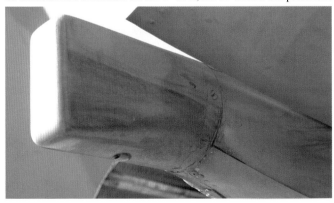

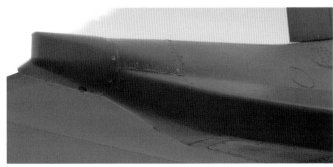

Above-- The F-15K has a couple noticeable modifications not found on its American F-15E counterpart. The CFT stations are slightly different, with an extended rear portion, while the formation strip lights behind the wings are of the newer, NVG-compatible type. Also visible are the exhausts of the General Electric F110-GE-129 engines that the South Koreans have chosen to power the F-15K.

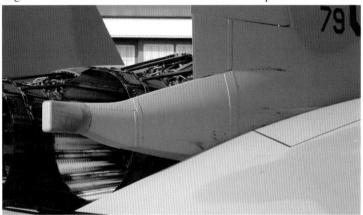

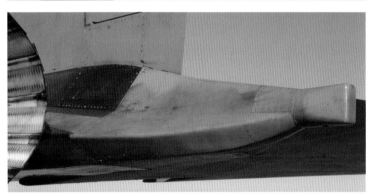

Different types of tailboom antenna are pictured above. At left is the F-15A, with no antenna. Middle and right photos depict the current F-15E configuration. Some export customers, notably the Israelis and South Koreans, have opted to mount additional chaff/flare dispensers on the bottom of the tailboom of their Eagles, below left. These are not found on any USAF versions, below right.

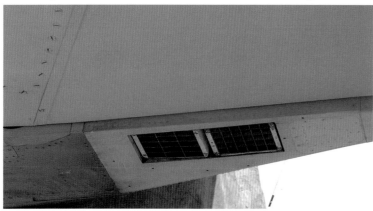

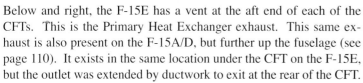

Below and right, the F-15E has a vent at the aft end of each of the CFTs. This is the Primary Heat Exchanger exhaust. This same exhaust is also present on the F-15A/D, but further up the fuselage (see page 110). It exists in the same location under the CFT on the F-15E, but the outlet was extended by ductwork to exit at the rear of the CFT.

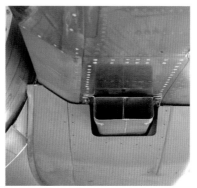

An emergency arrestor hook is located between the two engines at the aft end of the jet, above and below right. Very early F-15A-D models had a fairing built around the hook to reduce drag in that area, above and above right. However, the fairing was removed by the early 1990s and never installed on the F-15E.

Above-- The interior of the engine exhausts are coated with a white ceramic material. However, due to the intense heat of this area, the ceramic doesn't stay white for long. The black, sooty, streaks become more pronounced as the engine ages.

A pair of Pratt & Whitney engines powers all USAF Eagle models as well as most export versions. The first Eagles relied on the F100-PW-100 engine. This model, however, had many problems and was soon replaced in the late-model F-15C/D by the slightly upgraded -220 model--now with DEEC (Digital Electronic Engine Control). This engine is an improvement over the original -100. It offers increased reliability, better performance, and improved economy. Although some -100 engines remain in use, most F-15A/B/C/D models, and many F-15Es, are powered by the -220. However, to counter the F-15E's increased weight and parasite drag, the new F100-PW-229 Increased

Performance Engine (IPE) was installed beginning on F-15E 90-0233. All later Strike Eagles have the -229 engine installed. This holds true for many export versions of the Strike Eagle, as well, including the Israeli F-15I Ra'am. This engine features greatly improved reliability, economy, and more thrust. On USAF Strike Eagles, there are no external differences visible from outside the jet, but the -229 has a different nose cone on the engine front, right, than the -100 or -220 engine, left. However, on the F-15I, the engine turkey feathers have a distinctive metallic black sheen to them, identical to that found on Block 52 F-16s.

 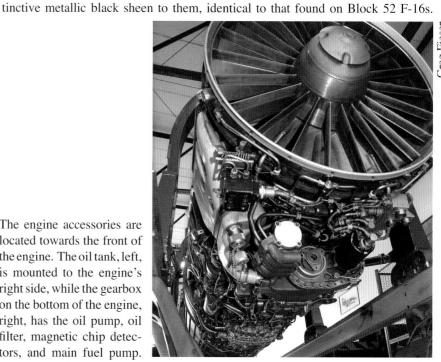

The engine accessories are located towards the front of the engine. The oil tank, left, is mounted to the engine's right side, while the gearbox on the bottom of the engine, right, has the oil pump, oil filter, magnetic chip detectors, and main fuel pump.

To further reduce maintenance issues, the turkey feathers, shown installed above left, were removed by the early 1980's from all USAF machines. Early problems were created by turbulent airflow between the exhausts during high AOA flight. As a result, the turkey feathers would sometimes separate from the aircraft in flight due to unforeseen stresses on the turkey feather attachment points. It was deemed easier to remove the turkey feathers than to try to correct the airflow problem. The resultant drag is of little consequence. Most foreign users of the jet have had their turkey feathers removed, as well, with the exception of the Israelis. Most Eagles in their inventory remain equipped with their engines' turkey feathers.

Another difference between the -100/220 engine and the -229 is the interior of the exhaust. The -229, below left, has a different afterburner flameholder than the -100/220, below right.

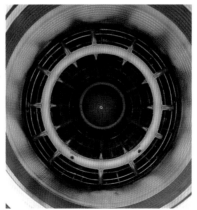

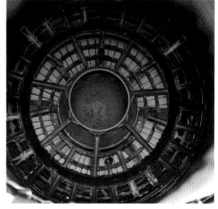

The South Koreans opted for the General Electric F110-GE-129 engines in their F-15K, as did the Republic of Singapore Air Force for use in their F-15SG, left and below. These are the first and only Eagle variants to use the GE engine operationally. Each of these engines produces 29,400 lbs. thrust.

Darren Mottram

A closer look at the exhaust nozzle is available left and above. Each of the exhaust nozzle plates is linked together by interlocking links, actuators, and pushrods.

The engines are faired into the fuselage by titanium paneling. Note the slight difference in this paneling between the F-15E, below, and the F-15A-D, above and below left. The F-15E does not have the U-shaped indentation at the bottom of the engine.

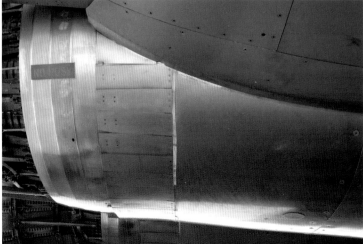

Although the hook remains identical for all Eagle models, the hook fairing is different. The F-15E's hook, left, is extended down by two inches from the bottom of the fuselage to make space available for internal avionics. The arrestor hook on the F-15A-D is flush with the bottom of the fuselage.

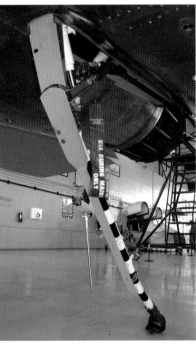

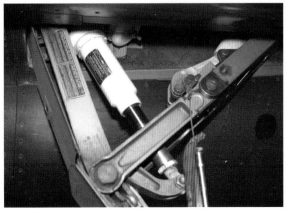

Greg Fieser

The engines are interchangeable from left to right, which saves both time and money. If everything goes perfectly, an engine can be removed, replaced, and the aircraft returned to service by a team of 3-4 in as little as four hours, including a test run and operations check. The ducts on the bulkhead are ECS bleed air crossover lines that transfer bleed air from the right Primary Heat Exchanger to join the air leaving the left exchanger enroute to the Air Cycle Air Conditioning System (ACACS, or Secondary Heat Exchanger).

Right-- The Engine is held in place in the airfame by way of a three-way mount: two on the side and one on top. The side mounts (sometimes called "coke bottles," due to their shape) slide into a recess on the sides of the engine, then lock in place using "jaws" that close on the other end of the mounts. The top mount is a pin with an interlink that is attached to the top of the fuselage that drops down into a U-shaped frame on the engine. The engine mount "jaws" can be seen at right on both sides of the engine bay. The silver upper mount is also visible on the top of the bay hanging near the bulkhead.

Greg Fieser

Greg Fieser

Jake Melampy

USAF

The fuselage surrounding the engines and engine bays, with the exception of the tailhook cover, is made from high-temperature titanium. The color of the titanium varies widely depending on a number of factors, including age of the airframe, flying hours, maintenance or lack thereof, etc. Some aircraft with a particularly dedicated crewchief have this area polished to a high degree of shine. The titanium paneling extends outwards to the bottom of the fuselage adjacent to the engines, as well, below. The stabilator actuator, bottom right, is in this area. It lives under an access panel between the engines and stabilators, below right.

Greg Fieser

Greg Fieser

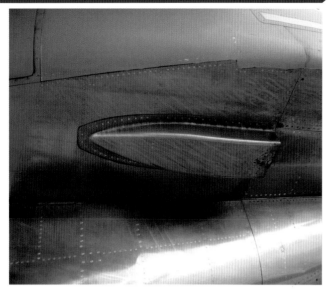

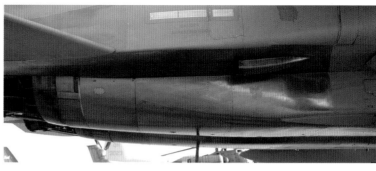

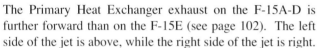

The Primary Heat Exchanger exhaust on the F-15A-D is further forward than on the F-15E (see page 102). The left side of the jet is above, while the right side of the jet is right.

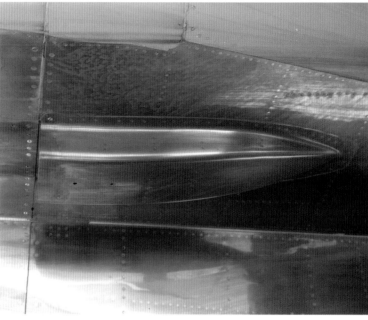

Left and right-- The wings blend into the fuselage above the fuselage missile stations. On the underside of each wing joint are a couple vents. The forward inlet is a ram air inlet for additional engine cooling. Behind this is the Primary Heat Exchanger inlet. Further aft is the Primary Heat Exchanger exhaust. The left side of the jet is pictured at right, while the jet's right side is pictured at left and below left.

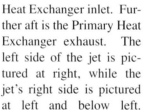

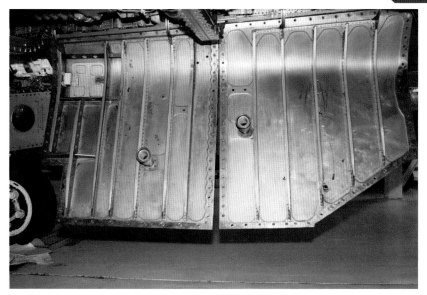

The majority of the bottom of the fuselage opens up to facilitate engine mainte-nance. Pictured is the left engine and its doors; the right side is a mirror image. Both doors pictured above open to expose the engine's gearbox/accessories. The bottom left photo is the very front of the engine. Mounted to the gearbox here are the oil pump, oil filter, magnetic chip detectors, and main fuel pump.

The tube with the hole is the breather pressurizing valve, which mates to a similar tube integral to the bottom engine bay door, above left. The bottom right photo shows the next access door back, which reveals the fuel control unit. The -100 engine uses a Unified Control (UFC), but the -220/-229 engines both use a Main Fuel Control (MFC), pictured here. The MFC works in conjunction with DEEC inputs. In both bot-tom two photos, the front of the jet is towards the left.

The photos at left and right show the jet's centerline, normally hidden by the weapons pylon that lives here (station 5). At left, the front of the jet is at the bottom, while at right, the front of the jet is at the top. The large round hole visible at left is the exhaust for the Eagle's Jet Fuel Starter (JFS). The JFS is a small gas turbine jet engine used to start the jet's engines during normal operations. It can also be used in an emergency situation to re-start the Eagle's engines up to altitudes of 20,000 feet. The JFS exhaust is examined more closely below. The photo at left is the original exhaust with the louvers. The F-15E, however, has no louvers, below right. By 1994, all remaining F-15A-D Eagles had their exhaust modified to the new, louver-less type.

The F-15 is equipped with a fire extinguishing system to give the aircrew an opportunity to put out a fire while still in the air. The system consists of a storage bottle, left, aft of the JFS exhaust, titanium discharge lines, electrically discharged cartridges, and fire/overheat sensing loops. The sensing element loops can detect a fire situation in the forward sections of each engine bay, JFS and AMAD compartments, and the afterburner sections of each engine bay. The extinguishing agent can be directed into these sensing element zones depending on the situation. In the cockpit, a FIRE warning light will illuminate to inform the aircrew of a potential fire problem. Once the pilot pushes the FIRE light, the electrical discharge cartridges are armed, and through a relay, the bleed air and engine fuel shutoff valves close for the corresponding engine. Activating the DISCHARGE switch fires the discharge cartridge, which breaks the seal on the storage bottle, releasing fire extinguishing agent into the engine bay. The process is similar for an AMAD/JFS compartment fire, except the fuel shutoff and bleed air valves are not closed.

Right-- The AMADs (Airframe Mounted Accessory Drive) are mounted to the airframe on either side of the CGB. Although they are physically bolted to the airframe, they connect to the engines' gearbox to drive the Eagle's hydraulic pumps (Utility and Power Control) and generator. In addition, they transfer JFS power to the engines for start. Visible in these two photos is the generator. Both hydraulic pumps are largely blocked from view.

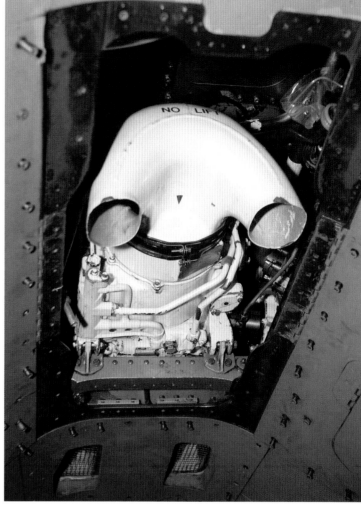

The JFS works hand-in-hand with the Central Gear Box (CGB). The CGB mates with and is forward of the JFS. It has its own intake system to keep itself cool. The intake system, called baby pants, is at the forward end of the CGB, above and left. Inputs from the JFS are used to drive the CGB. As the CGB is powered up, numerous other systems come on-line, including the AMAD, below and below left, which is designed to transfer power from the CGB/JFS to the engines' gearbox to start each engine. Left is a general overview of the bottom of the CGB. The front of the jet is at the left of the photo. Above, the front of the jet is at the top of the photo. The two small vents behind the CGB are the air intake inlets for the JFS. Above left, the panels that normally cover this area have been removed, allowing a glimpse of the bottom of the JFS.

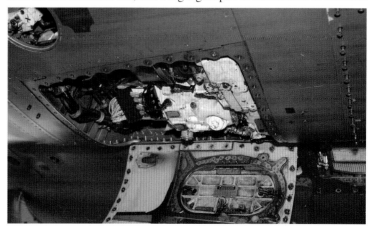

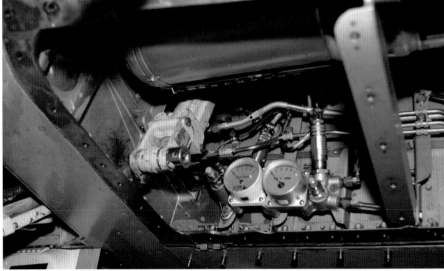

The JFS accumulator bottles, left, store hydraulic fluid under pressure that is used to start the JFS and operate emergency systems (emergency gear extension, for example). There are two accumulator bottles. Both bottles use an internal piston to provide air pressure against the hydraulic fluid to build pressure. Each bottle has enough fluid and pressure for one JFS start. The pressure gauges, above, display pressure inside the accumulators. The accumulators are on the bottom of the fuselage, immediately aft of the left main landing gear. The front of the jet is up in the photo at left, and to the left in the photo above.

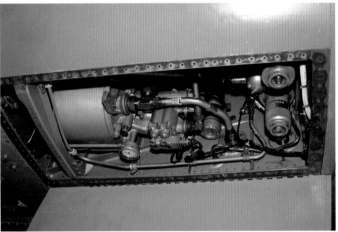

Three separate hydraulic systems make up the F-15's systems. Four hydraulic pumps, mounted to the AMAD, provide pressure for the systems. Each system (Power Control 1 and Power Control 2 --PC1/PC2-- and Utility) has its own reservoir for fluid storage. Each system supplies hydraulic power to separate parts of the aircraft. PC1 and PC2 power the flight controls (ailerons, rudders, and horizontal stabilators). PC1 powers the left side; PC2, the right. The Utility system is the largest. It provides hydraulic power to the rest of the aircraft--landing gear, brakes, canopy, speed brake, nose wheel steering, radar, JFS accumulators, intake ramps, emergency generator, etc. System redundancy is built into each system to allow an alternate source of hydraulic power to a system that is not operating correctly. The PC system filters and fluid reservoirs are pictured above. They are located inboard of the main landing gear. The Utility reservoir is left, along with its filters. The reservoir holds 4.1 gallons of fluid, vs. the 1.4 gallons in the PC reservoirs. The Utility reservoir's location is on the bottom of the fuselage, behind the right main landing gear, and outboard of the JFS accumulator bottles. Missile rail station 6 is partly visible.

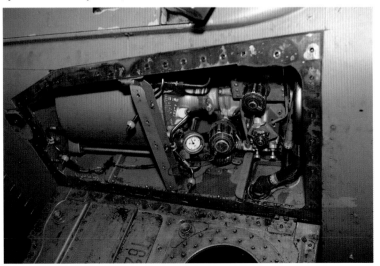

Forward of the main landing gear, the Eagle's belly is much less cluttered. Loading of the internal gun takes place on the belly, immediately forward of the centerline pylon.

The F-15E's gun loading door, left and below, is slightly different than the door found on other Eagles. The F-15E has a smaller ammunition drum and redesigned ammunition belt. As a result of these changes, the gun door has a distinctive bulge to it.

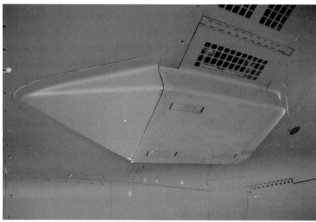

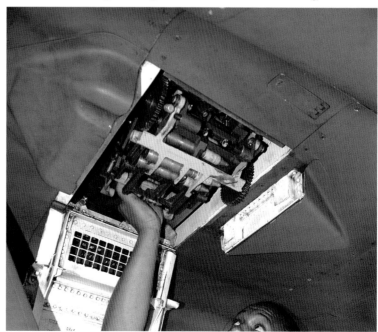

For self-protection, all Eagles are equipped with the AN/ALE-45 chaff/flare dispenser system. These are located on the bottom of each intake, immediately forward of the main landing gear wells and behind the F-15E's nav/targeting pods. Often during peacetime, the dispensers are removed from the jet and fairings are placed over the openings, as shown. The photo above left shows empty dispensers as well as the fairings.

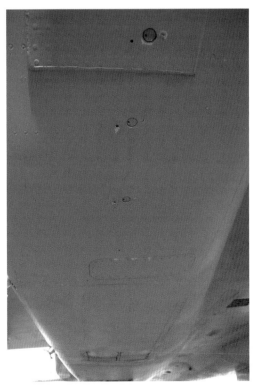

While the majority of the bottom of the Eagle is full of inspection doors, access covers, exhausts, and vents, the bottom of the intakes are relatively sparse. The jet's right intake is left, while the left intake is at right. Both photos are looking toward the rear of the jet. A ground check panel (sometimes also known as the "comm door") is located on the bottom of the left intake. It folds down when in use to allow the crewchief to communicate to the pilot during engine start. It also has provisions for various control functions, such as fuel system and bleed air tests. The F-15A/B door is above left. The F-15C/D introduced a different style door, which was carried over to the F-15E. It is the door shown above right.

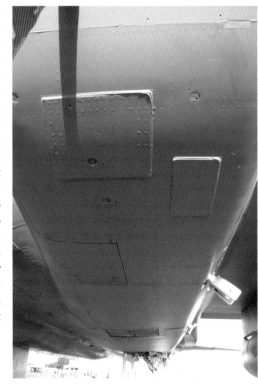

Most of the F-15's communications antenna are located on the forward fuselage bottom, aft of the radome and below the cockpit. At left is a modern jet's antenna configuration. From front to back, these antenna are the ICMS Band 3 AN/ALQ-135B nodule, combined UHF/VHF blade antenna, the ICMS (Internal Counter Measures System) Band 2 antenna, and lower IFF/UHF antenna. An identical AN/ALQ-135 Band 3 nodule is found on top of the fuselage behind the radome. These were installed relatively recently on most F-15Cs, and not found on F-15A/B/D or F-15E models. The Band 3 nodules are examined more closely below left. Likewise, the ICMS Band 2 antenna is detailed closely below right. The F-15E differs from the F-15C in that its ICMS antenna is flush-

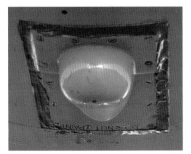

mounted to the bottom of the fuselage, above right, due to its different ICMS suite. It is worth pointing out that the F-15B and F-15D have no ICMS whatsoever due to the addition of the rear seat, which leaves no space for the ICMS equipment usually stored in Bay 5.

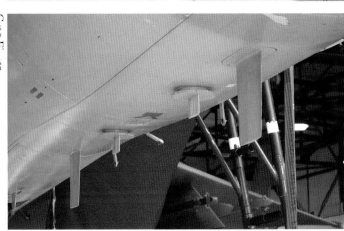

Over the years, there have been several types of UHF/VHF antenna configurations used. Some of the different styles can be found on this page and throughout the book. The original configuration is shown at left. The UHF antenna is at the front, followed by a pair of ICMS Band 2 antennas. The Eagle received the AN/ARC-210 secure voice UHF/VHF radio beginning in 2004, and the associated UHF/VHF antenna was replaced with a "shark fin" shaped antenna, above right, by 2006. Above left is another common antenna shape, often found on late F-15C/D and the F-15E. The F-15A/B is most often equipped with a straight, non-swept UHF antenna as shown at left. Installation of the Band 3 ICMS nodule required a slight shuffling of the antenna locations. The forward Band 2 antenna is removed, and the forward UHF antenna moved aft to make room for the Band 3 nodule. This configuration is shown above left and above right.

The F-15A through D models all share the same nose gear assembly, which retracts forward into the gear well. Considering the 59,000 pound maximum takeoff weight of the fully-loaded F-15C/D, the nose gear appears relatively scrawny. Gear retraction is powered by the jet's Utility hydraulic system. The nose gear drag brace is mounted to the forward portion of the gear strut, above the oleo. It folds in two as the gear is tucked into the wheel well. Mounted on the drag brace is a taxi light, while a larger landing light is mounted to the gear strut. Although seldom used, the factory included a pair of tiedown rings along both sides of the gear strut. Nose gear steering is provided via hydraulic pressure from the nosewheel steering unit on the top of the gear strut. The pilot steers the jet on the ground with the rudder pedals.

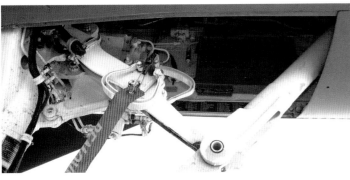

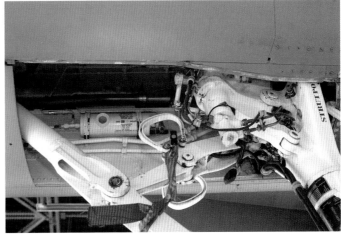

The cables that snake their way down the main strut are secured by clamps. The cables lead to the landing and taxi lights. One forward door and one aft door enclose the nose gear assembly during flight. The aft gear door is mechanically linked to the gear strut and opens/closes along with the gear, requiring no hydraulic assistance. The forward gear door, shown on page 121, is linked to the gear uplatch and door cylinder/mechanism.

The F-15E's undercarriage was strengthened to handle the Strike Eagle's increased weight. The nose gear wheel/tire assembly is thicker, while the strut fork is constructed of larger "I" shaped material vs. the smaller, rounded strut fork found on other Eagle models. In addition, the drag brace is thicker, as is the gear strut itself. Another change with the Strike Eagle gear is the wiring conduit that leads electrical cables from the jet down the strut to the landing and taxi lights. The apparatus sticking out from the oleo strut, right and below, is a shimmy dampener added in the late 1990's to reduce oscillations during high-speed taxi and/or takeoff and landing. It is found only on the Strike Eagle.

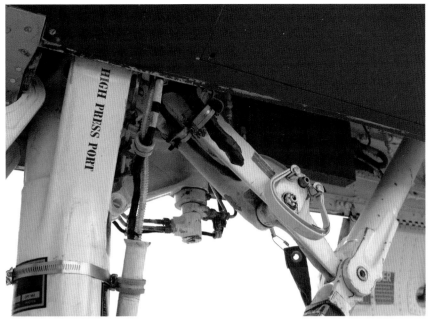

The forward nose gear door is home to the lower TACAN blade antenna. Just forward of this is the flush-mounted ILS marker beacon antenna. The inside of the door, below, shows signs of the antennas' presence in the form of wiring harnesses, which are secured to the door with clamps. All F-15 versions share the same door.

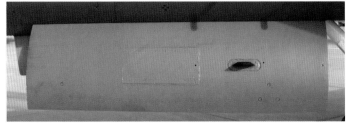

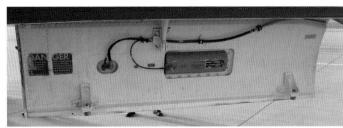

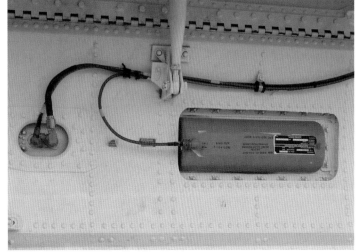

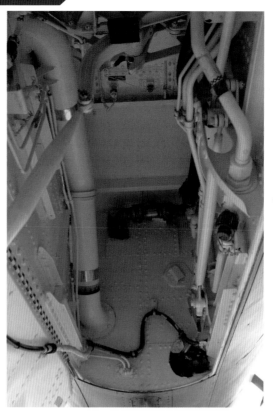

The nose gear tucks into a relatively tiny gear well. The well is situated directly beneath the cockpit floor, sandwiched on either side by the forward avionics bays. The gear retracts forward into the well, covered by two doors that fold closed. At left, the forward section of the gear is viewed, looking forward. In both instances, the front of the jet is down. The F-15A-D versions all have very similar wells. It is the well far left. The F-15E, however, is a fairly radical departure. It features large pipes and hoses that deliver cooling air from the Heat Exchangers used to cool the radar and its associated avionics. One such pipe is clearly visible at left on the left side of the well, disappearing into the well's forward bulkhead.

All three photos below show the wells viewed looking aft. The rear of the jet, and wheel well, is at the bottom of each photo. The nose gear's upper drag brace is visible in each photo, as is the nose gear retraction strut near the rear bulkhead. It connects to the nose gear shock strut to pull it into the well during retraction, and to push it down during extension. The forward nose gear door is partially visible on the right of each photo. The linkage that connects to it leads to the NLG uplatch and door mechanism. This device is just forward of the upper drag brace attach point in the floor of the well. It locks the nose gear up in the well during flight, and, through the mechanical linkage, also opens/closes the forward gear door. The forward gear door normally remains closed on the ground. However, it can be manually opened for inspection, maintenance, or, in this instance, photographs. Again, the Strike Eagle has a different well than earlier Eagle models. The F-15A-D well is below left. The two remaining photos depict the F-15E.

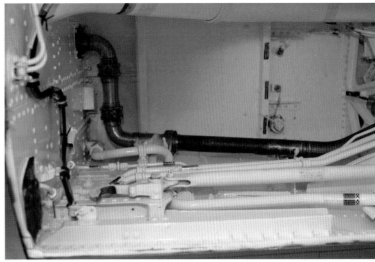

The top of the gear well is above, left, and below left. The F-15E's added avionics cooling piping is again visible above and below left. The F-15A-D is directly left. Mounted to the left wall is the grey Avionics Status Panel (ASP). As the name implies, the ASP monitors the jet's avionics systems for malfunctions during flight. Each of the black windows on the side of the box will have an orange tag visible if that system experienced a malfunction during flight. The jet's crew-chief uses this box to quickly identify any potential avionics anomalies.

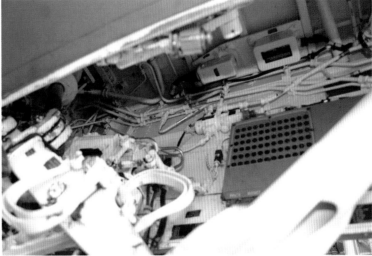

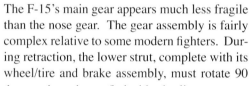

The F-15's main gear appears much less fragile than the nose gear. The gear assembly is fairly complex relative to some modern fighters. During retraction, the lower strut, complete with its wheel/tire and brake assembly, must rotate 90 degrees in order to fit inside the limited confines of the gear wells. This is accomplished using torque arms, that, among other things, transmit a turning force onto the lower strut. The torque arms can be seen below, connecting the upper and lower gear strut.

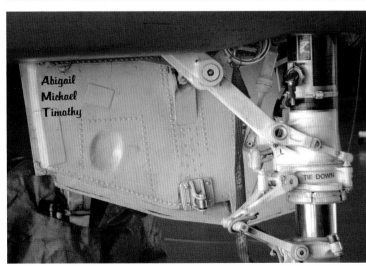

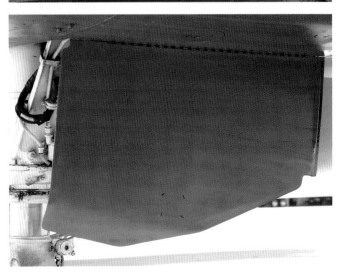

Like the nose gear, the main gear of the F-15E is strengthened, too. The gear strut is substantially thicker to cope with the Strike Eagle's heavier gross weight. The drag brace, below right, is wider and thicker. The drag springs (the round springs mounted to the drag braces) are larger in diameter to help the heavier strut retract. More noticeable is the larger wheel and tire assembly, next page. Above left, cabling is visible snaking its way from the jet down to the brakes. These are electrical cables to feed the Anti-Skid system. The Anti-Skid Brake system works to prevent the wheels from locking-up on slippery runways. If the system detects one wheel moving more slowly than the rest, brake pressure is decreased on that wheel to prevent lock-up. This makes the jet far easier to control during rainy weather.

Below right-- The gear is pushed out of the well during the retraction sequence by the gear actuator. It is the large cylinder to the right (inboard) of the landing gear drag brace. Hydraulic pressure from the jet's Utility system forces a large piston inside the actuator to move inside the cylinder, forcing the actuator strut to move in/out to move the gear strut.

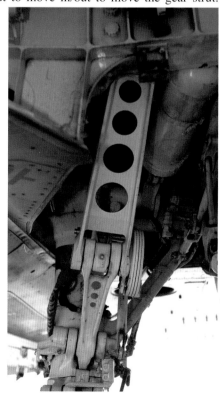

Although the Strike Eagle's wheel pattern remains the same as the "light grey" versions, the wheel of the F-15E is noticeably wider to accommodate the increased weight of the jet. Likewise, the brakes were beefed up as well. Like the landing gear, the Utility hydraulic system provides pressure for normal brake operations. Should this fail, emergency braking is available by releasing stored hydraulic pressure from the JFS accumulators.

A Remove Before Flight tag/pin, left, is used to safe the gear when the jet is on the ground. It is inserted into each jury link.

Below and below left-- Note the different internal detail of the F-15E's gear doors vs. that found on the F-15A-D.

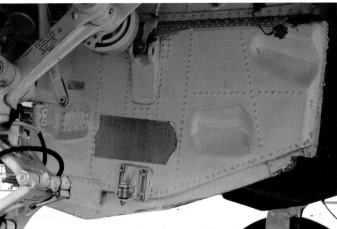

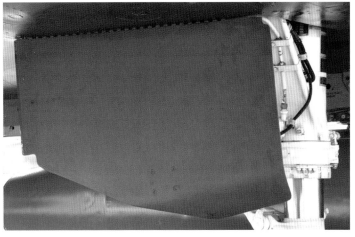

Greg Fieser

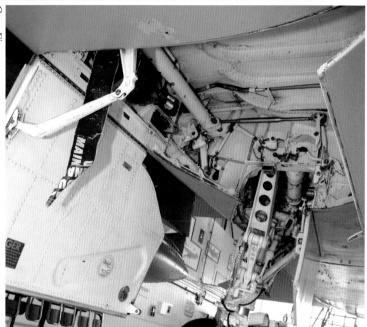

Three doors cover each main gear. The forward doors, like the nose gear doors, normally remain closed when the Eagle is on the ground, only opening for the extension/retraction sequence. Also like the nose gear doors, they can be opened manually by ground crew. The aft door remains open whenever the gear is down. All doors are mechanically opened/closed by linkages. This page details the wells found in the F-15A-D. The F-15E's wells are shown on the next page. The red cap visible in the right gear well on the inboard wall, below and below right, is the jet's defuel port.

Greg Fieser

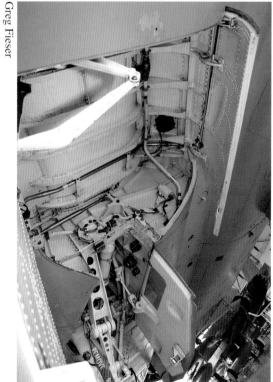

Jake Melampy

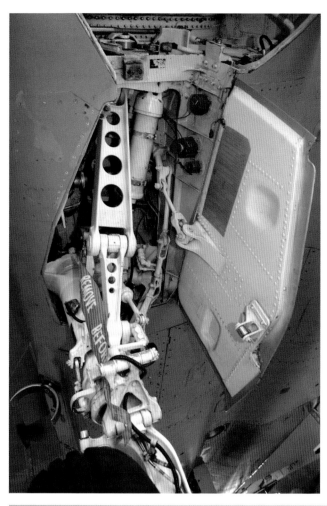

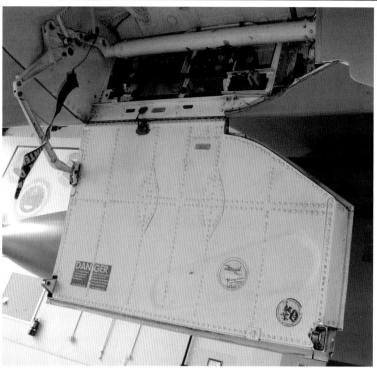

Greg Fieser

The aft gear well, left, is totally filled by the gear strut, drag brace, and retraction strut. Its gear door is open at all times the gear is down, unlike the forward main gear bays. The right outboard door is pictured above. Below, the gear retraction sequence is almost complete as this 57th Wing F-15C blasts out of Nellis AFB, Nevada for a Weapons School sortie. The main gear are nearly completely tucked into their wells, followed closely by the nose gear. The doors will close in a matter of seconds.

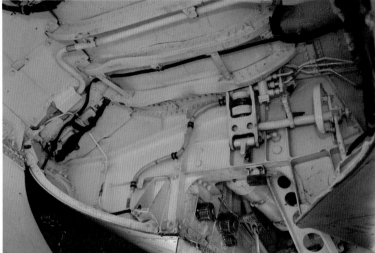

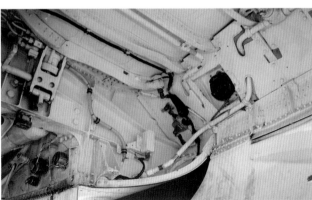

While not significantly different, there are a few subtle changles present in the F-15E's wheel wells. The forward bay's aft bulkhead, above, has a different pattern than was seen inside the well of the F-15A-D. The red defuel fitting is still present on the inboard wall of the right well, left. In all versions of the jet, the ouboard wall of each well is cluttered with electrical wiring, relays, and circuit breakers. The left well is below, and the right well is below left. The aft main well, meanwhile, is almost totally consumed by the gear strut, drag brace, and gear actuator. The red caps on the wall of the well are hydraulic system servicing ports.

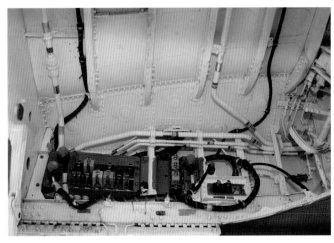

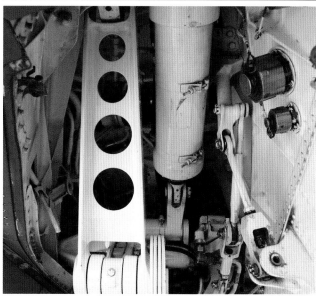

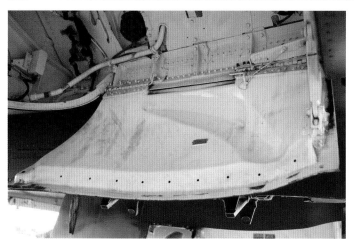

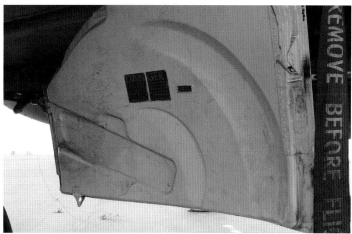

Weapons Pylons

In addition to the F-15E's CFT pylons and the AIM-7 integral launch rails of the F-15A-D, all Eagles have a single wing pylon under each wing, as well as a centerline pylon strapped to the bottom of the fuselage. Each wing pylon can then mount a pair of air-air missile rails, allowing a total load of eight air-air missiles. The wing pylons are the same from the F-15A-D to the F-15E, with the exception of the addition of the BRU-47/A bomb release unit to the F-15E. The BRU-47 is equipped with the necessary wiring to carry and drop precision-guided weapons such as JDAMs in addition to regular dumb bombs and external fuel tanks.

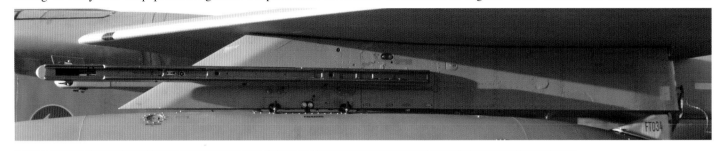

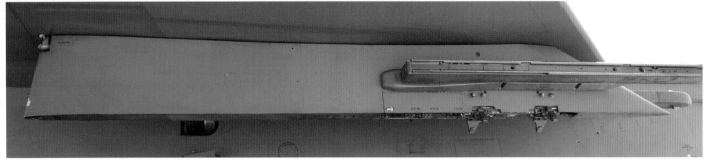

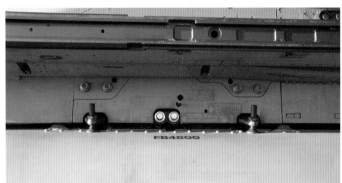

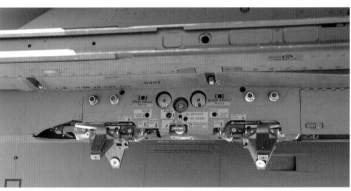

Above and above right-- The F-15E's BRU-47/A is pictured above right, while the F-15A-D's MAU-12 is above left. The MAU-12 has the ability to carry an external fuel tank, as pictured, but cannot drop the precision-guided weapons that the BRU-47/A is able to.

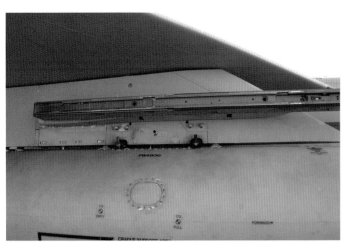

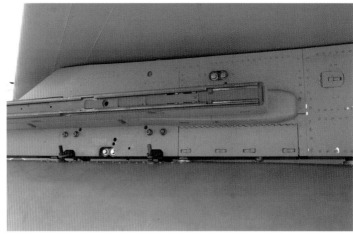

A pair of missile rails is mounted to each wing pylon, above. In this instance, this particular Eagle has the new LAU-128 rails fitted, which are compatible with the AIM-120 and AIM-9X missiles. The small silver ball, left and below, is to aid in separation from the jet in the event of pylon jettisoning, resulting in a clean separation from the aircraft. The small hole in the rear of the pylon, right, is a fuel vent for the external fuel tanks. Above that is a grounding port.

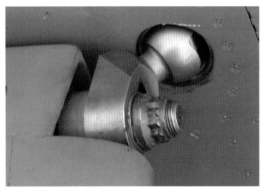

The centerline pylon is nearly identical to the wing pylons. As is the case with the wing pylons, the F-15E uses the BRU-47/A bomb release unit, while other Eagles use the MAU-12. The centerline pylon has the same silver swivel ball to aid jettisoning that is present on the wing pylon.

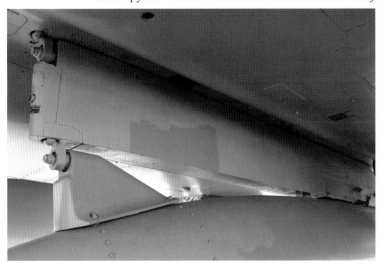

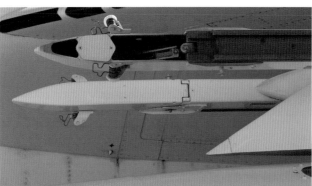

The AIM-9 Sidewinder family of air-air missiles are carried on the shoulder stations of each wing pylon. The LAU-114 missile rail was fitted to all F-15s as the jets left the factory in St. Louis. The rail is fitted to the pylon via an adaptor unit. Notice how the front of each rail has a spring that folds behind the forward fin of the AIM-9, below. This missile rail can only be used with an ACMI pod or an AIM-9. Israeli jets use use the LAU-7I for AIM-9 carriage, which also allows them to carry their Python III/IV.

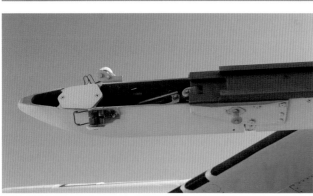

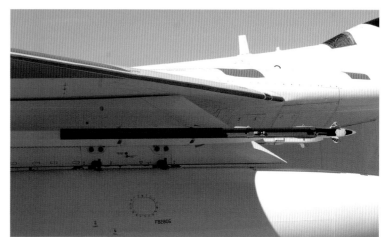

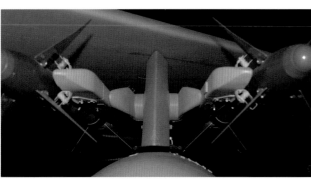

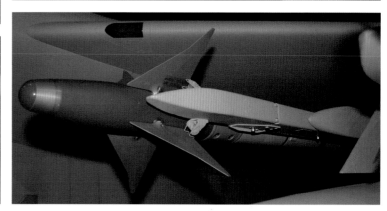

With the introduction of the AIM-120 AMRAAM into USAF service in 1991, it was necessary to fit all F-15s with new rails that were compatible with the new missile. The LAU-128 rails were gradually fitted to the Eagle community beginning in 1992. Initially, only two rails were fitted at a time, usually on the outboard stations of the wing pylons. However, by the mid- to late-1990s, most USAF Eagles had been fitted with four LAU-128 rails, entirely eliminating the older, Sidewinder-only, LAU-106 rails. It is still possible, however, for foreign users of the Eagle, especially JASDF and IADF/AF, to carry a pair of LAU-128s and a pair of the older LAU-106s. The LAU-128 is compatible with the AIM-9M, AIM-9X, AIM-120, and ACMI pod.

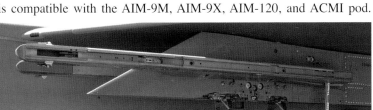

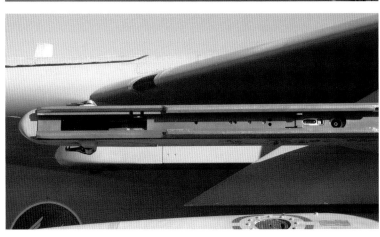

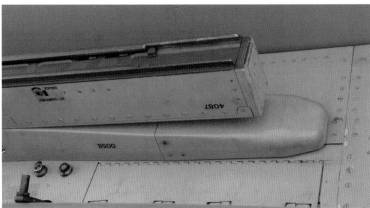

In addition to the new rails, the rail adaptors, left and below, were changed with the addition of the LAU-128. The new adaptors, ADU-552, are shorter than their predecessors.

Ken Middleton

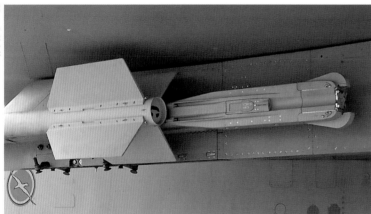

Ken Middleton

The AN/ALE-58 BOL dispenser is a chaff and infrared dispenser designed to fit on the tail end of the LAU-128 missile rail. Each BOL dispenser holds 160 countermeasures packages released through a non-pyrotechnic mechanism. They are dispersed into the airflow behind the Eagle using the jet's vortices to distribute the countermeasures more effectively. It is funded by the Air National Guard, and found only on their F-15A-D model Eagles. Typically, only the ouboard missile rails will have the BOL dispenser present. Some ANG units have carried them on the inboard rails, especially when an AIM-9X is carried on the outboard rails as compatibility testing of the AIM-9X and the BOL rails has not been done,

Ken Middleton

Up to three external fuel tanks can be carried by the Eagle to extend the jet's range. Although the centerline pylon is capable of carrying a fuel tank, it is most common for a pair of tanks to be carried from the wing pylons, rather than a single tank mounted to the centerline. The external tanks each hold 600 gallons of fuel. The capacity of each tank is actually 610 gallons, but extra space is allotted for fuel expansion. Air pressure from the ECS pressurizes the external tanks and transfers the fuel into the internal tanks as the internal system needs it.

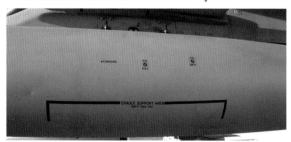

USAF

Above right-- "Nestable" fuel tanks are quickly-constructed fuel tanks used during wartime. They were originally designed for the F-15A and C models. They are not as rigidly contructed as the regular external tanks, since they are not meant to be used for long periods of time. They are shipped to the deployment area in pieces and assembled there, so they take up less space during transport. They are identical in appearance to a standard external tank, with the exception of the rear end, which is decidedly flat. They also remain in FS 36375 paint, making a strong contrast to the Mod Eagle scheme now carried by the F-15A-D, and the dark 36118 paint of the F-15E, as shown.

137

The AIM-7 Sparrow had been the USAF's medium-range missile of choice for the better part of half a century. It remains in service with the US Navy, although it has largely been phased out of service with the USAF in favor of the newer AIM-120 AMRAAM. The Eagle used the AIM-7F version of the Sparrow, which entered service in 1976, followed by the AIM-7M, entering service in 1982. It was the AIM-7M that proved so successful against Iraqi fighters during Operation Desert Storm in 1991, scoring 22 kills in the short period of conflict. The -7F was usually painted gloss white, while the -7M was light ghost grey. Common to all air-air missiles, yellow and brown bands signify a live weapon in contrast to the training/inert weapon's blue bands. Four Sparrows can be mounted along the bottom of the fuselage via LAU-106 missile rails built into the Eagle's fuselage bottom. Notice that the bands do not cover the conduits along the body of the missile. It is also worth pointing out that the guidance fins are not painted black, but rather a natural, unpainted metal.

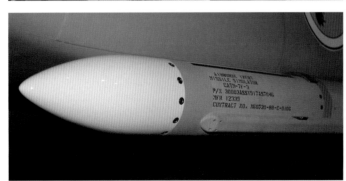

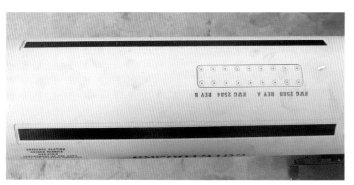

Above-- To provide proximity fuzing, the Sparrow is equipped with an external fuze towards the missile's head. The AIM-7F has two such fuzes, while the AIM-7M, above, has four.

Right and below-- The missile's guidance fins are normally left off of the missile until it is installed onto the jet. The green port serves as the electrical connection between jet and missile.

Above-- The CATM-7 is an inert training shape used to simulate the feel of an AIM-7 for pilots during training missions. It can be carried with or without guidance fins. It will always have blue stripes to signify its inert status. Notice the difference of the aft end of the CATM-7 vs. the live AIM-7, below.

139

Although introduced into the USAF in 1991, the AIM-120 didn't arrive in-theatre in time to see significant use during Operation Desert Storm. It wasn't until the summer of 1992 that it saw widespread use on F-15s and F-16s over the Gulf, scoring its first kill in 1992 (although fired from an F-16D). It has since all but entirely replaced the vintage AIM-7 Sparrow medium-range missile. The AMRAAM (Advanced Medium Range Air-Air Missile) is a radar-guided missile with "fire-and-forget" ability, meaning it can be launched and left to its own to search out its target, with no further input from the launch aircraft. With its 30 nautical mile range, it truly has BVR (Beyond Visual Range) capability, giving the Eagle a true advantage over its target when paired with the APG-70 radar. Three version of the AMRAAM are now in use. The original AIM-120A was introduced in 1988, and it was joined by the AIM-120B and AIM-120C a few years later. The AIM-120C can be distinguished by its smaller control surfaces. Up to eight AMRAAMs can be carried at a time by the Eagle. Four can be carried on the built-in fuselage stations, while an additional four can be mounted to the wing pylons' missile rails. When mounted to the wings, the AIM-120 requires the beefier LAU-128 rails. It cannot be carried by the original LAU-114. Typically, only two are carried on the wing stations at a time. On the F-15E, the AIM-120 is usually mounted to the outboard rails (2A and 8B), while on F-15A-D models, the AIM-120 is mounted to the inboard missile rails (stations 2B and 8A).

The live AIM-120 features a differently-shaped nose cone than its counterpart on the CATM-120, next page. The CATM-120 nose cone is much more blunt when compared to the sleeker, pointier nose on the live missile, above. Similarly, the rear ends of the AIM-120 vary greatly from the live missile to the CATM-120. The live AIM-120 has a bowl-shaped exhaust area, below left, while the rear end of the captive-carry CATM-120 features a flat rear end, below. Notice that the missiles' control surfaces are normally stored separately from the missile and only installed after the missile is loaded onto the jet. The control surfaces remain in a box, next page, until the time of installation onto the missile.

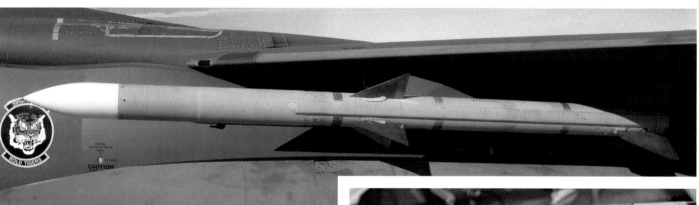

The AIM-120C, top of this page, is identified by its clipped control surfaces which were originally designed to fit into the small confines of the F-22 Raptor's weapons bays. The AIM-120B, above, has the original control surfaces. Both missiles above are captive-carry training shapes. The blue bands signify that both the rocket motor and explosive warhead are inert.

USAF

The AIM-9 Sidewinder has been in use with the Eagle since the beginning. Several versions of the missile have been used, from the AIM-9P of the early 1980's up to the AIM-9L of Desert Storm, to the AIM-9M of today. Up to four can be carried on the wing pylon's missile rails (stations 2A/B and 8A/B). Live missiles (this page) will be painted FS 36375, and can be identified by the yellow and brown bands. Inert training missiles can be painted FS 36375, white, various shades of blue, or any combination of all three. They have blue bands. The missile is armed by a small T-shaped handle midway along the missile's body (this page, bottom left).

Dave Roof

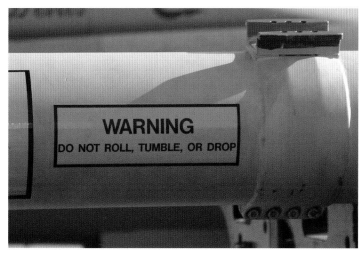

Dave Roof

The Captive Air Training Missile (CATM, left and below) does not have the steering rollerons on the rear fins as the live missile does. Also note the different rear ends of the missile between the "plug" on the CATM-9 at left and the rocket exhaust on the AIM-9 at far left. Additionally, the CATM-9 lacks the fuze band behind the seeker head that is present on the live AIM-9M, above right.

USAF

The AIM-9X is the newest generation of the Sidewinder family. It features "fire and forget" and high off-boresight capability, along with a greater acquisition range. It uses passive IR (InfraRed) energy for tracking, which can be used nearly at BVR range and close in. The -9X model has an extremely agile body due to its thrust vectoring control that results in a very maneuverable, reliable, and accurate missile. It was introduced to the USAF in 2002, and immediately hung from Eagles. It has slowly been replacing the AIM-9M on all "light grey" jets, although the F-15E currently lacks AIM-9X capability. It can only be carried on the wing stations, and only on the LAU-128 rail. The missile "talks" to the jet via an umbilical cord between the forward fins, as shown below. The cord connects to a wire harness inside the missile rail.

Dave Roof

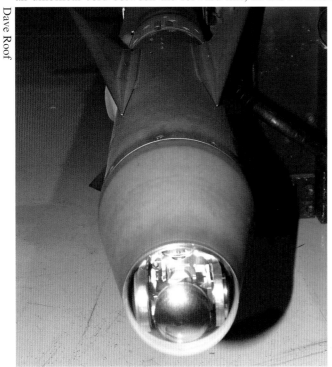

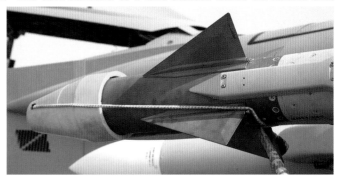

(Right) As with the AIM-9M model, the AIM-9X is armed prior to takeoff by a small lever along the missile's body. The lever is rotated counter-clockwise 180 degrees up to arm the missile, allowing it to be fired. It is once again rotated to "Safe" upon the jet's landing.

(Below) The missile is slid onto the missile rail via a pair of hangars on the missile's body. The hangars correspond with grooves inside the missile rails.

(Bottom) The thrust-vectoring system makes for a unique rear end to the missile. However, captive training missiles (CATM-9X) have only a flat rear end with no exhaust or vector plates.

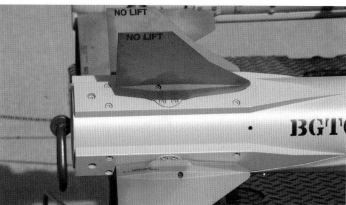

The ACMI (Air Combat Maneuvering and Instrumentation) pod is used to relay information to ground controllers and commanders during training exercises. Also sometimes known as AIS (Airborne Instrumentation Sub-system) pods, each pod is the link between the controllers on the ground and the individual aircraft carrying the pod. Each pod is exceptionally advanced and carries a number of sensors. Each sensor provides data for the controller and debrief system on the ground. The pod is able to generate an extremely accurate picture of the aircraft over the range down to within 15 feet due to modern GPS technology in real time. Information transmitted is also recorded for later play-back during the mass de-briefing after the flight. On the Eagle, the pod is carried on either of the wing pylons, usually on the outboard missile rail (station 2B or 8A).

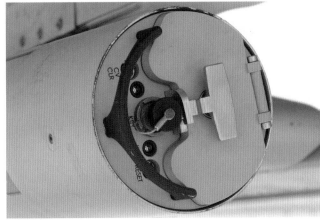

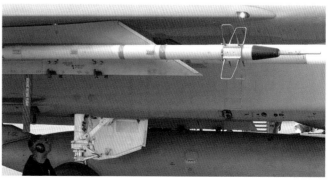

There are several versions of ACMI pods in use. Each has a slightly different function, tailored for the capabilities of the specific range where it is used. At left, the white pods are telemetry pods often carried by test Eagles at locations such as Eglin AFB, Florida, and Edwards AFB, California.

The JDAM kit consists of a tail section with integrated aerodynamic control surfaces, a stabilizing strake kit, and a combined Inertial Navigation System (INS) and GPS guidance control unit. JDAM enables accurate delivery against high priority targets from high altitudes in any weather. The 2,000lb GBU-31 first entered service in 2001, and saw heavy use in Operations Enduring Freedom, then again in 2003 during Operation Iraqi Freedom. It is based on the Mk. 84 series gravity bomb. It can be hung from stations 2/8, 5, and each of the CFT pylons (LCT/RCT 1, 2, an 3, although not simultaneously). The blue bombs at left and above denote inert training weapons. A variation to the standard GBU-31 is the GBU-31 (V) 3/B JDAM that replaces the Mk. 84 bomb body with a BLU-109 in its place. This results in a weapon able to penetrate hardened shelters and bunkers with the precision of the original JDAM. The bottom four photos of this page represent GBU-31 (V) 3/B version. The overall shape of the weapon is different, along with redesigned strakes. The aft tailkit, however, remains identical to the standard GBU-31.

The GBU-38 is the 500lb JDAM based on the Mk. 82 series gravity bombs. Like the GBU-31, it consists of a stabilizing kit on the nose, Inertial Navigation System (INS), a GPS guidance control unit, and movable rear fins to steer it towards its target. It was introduced to the F-15E in 2005 and is now in widespread use during missions over Iraq and Afghanistan. The GBU-38 may be mounted to the Strike Eagle on all hardpoints and pylon stations.

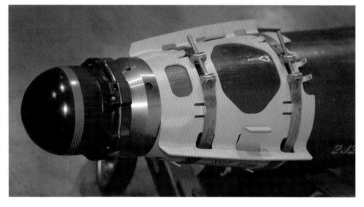

The GBU-12 is a laser-guided precision weapon based on the 500lb. Mk. 82 series bomb. Tracking a laser signal generated from the F-15E's targeting pod (LANTIRN or Sniper), another aircraft, or from friendly personnel on the ground, the GBU-12 uses its forward guidance fins to steer itself to the target, with a high degree of precision. Up to nine can be carried at a time on the eight CFT stations as well as the centerline. The guidance section has had two different styles of seeker lenses over the years. At left is the original style with the smaller clear opening, while below left is the newer style with an orange plastic lens. Both are still in use; however, the original style's use is on the decline.

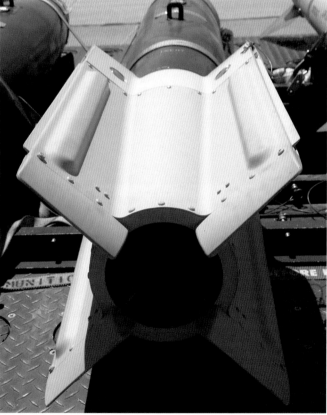

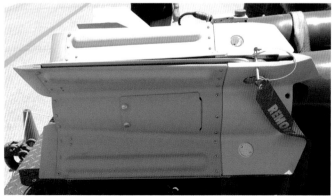

The GBU-24 is another laser-guided weapon, but based on the 2000lb Mk. 84 series bomb. It uses the same guidance kit as the GBU-12, as well as the same seeker head. It does, however, have larger guidance fins than the GBU-12. When carried, it is mounted to stations 2/8, 5, or the bottom CFT stations. It is worth pointing out that the guidance fins on all laser-guided bombs are color coded. GBU-12 fins have orange labels, below left, while the labels of the 2000 lb. GBU-10, below, are yellow. This is frequently in error on model decal sheets.

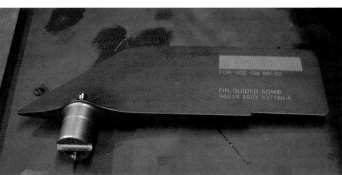

The GBU-24 consists of either a 2,000lb Mk. 84 general purpose or BLU-109 penetrator bomb modified with a Paveway III low-level laser-guided bomb kit. The BLU-109 type, shown below, is more common. The GBU-24 is carried on the same stations as the GBU-10.

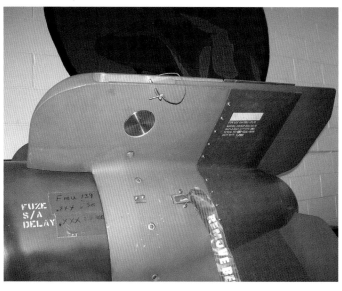

Known affectionately as the "Bunker Buster", the GBU-28 was originally developed in the mid-1990's to penetrate hardened underground targets. It is a massive 5,000lb weapon, modified from existing Army artillery tubes. It was developed as a direct result of operations during Operation Desert Storm in 1991 to destroy Iraqi underground shelters. Rushed to the theatre in the closing days of the conflict, two were successfully dropped from F-111s. They are still in the USAF inventory, but seldom loaded onto an aircraft, and rarely flown. When carried by the F-15E, it is loaded onto station 5 (the centerline).

USAF

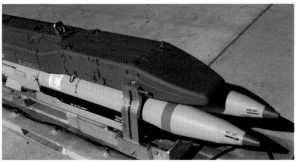

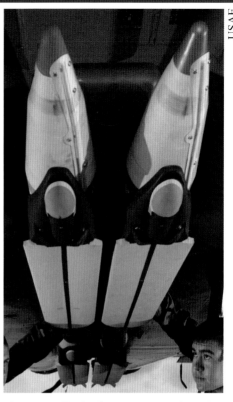

Perhaps the quintessential opposite of the GBU-28 Bunker Buster, the GBU-39 Small Diameter Bomb (SDB) is the smallest precision weapon in the USAF arsenal. Weighing in at just 285 pounds, the GBU-39 is a GPS-guided glide bomb designed as a direct result of recent operations in Iraq and Afghanistan. To minimize collateral damage, the GBU-39 was designed to carry a relatively small explosive warhead while improving existing precision parameters. It was first tested by the 40th Flight Test Squadron at Eglin AFB, Florida, in 2003. The first operational unit to use the SDB was the 48th Fighter Wing at RAF Lakenheath AB, England, in 2006. Four SDBs can be carried per station using a BRU-61 rack. The BRU-61/GBU-39 assembly can be carried from nine different stations. Both wings (stations 2/8), the centerline (station 5), and each of the lower CFT pylons are all wired to accept the GBU-39.

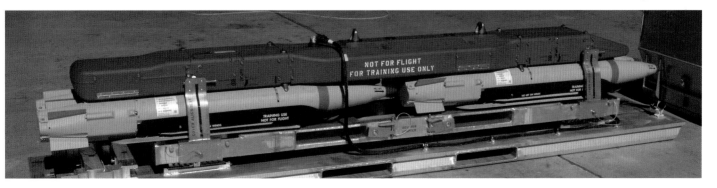

USAF

The EGBU-15 is a 2000lb weapon utilizing an electro-optical guidance unit via datalink control. It can be released at either very low or very high altitudes at very large distances. It is equipped with either an imaging infra-red seeker or a television unit that provides the F-15E with a visual reproduction of the target that is displayed on the cockpit's television monitor. The Strike Eagle's WSO (Weapons Systems Officer) can then manually steer the bomb onto the target or elect to lock the bomb onto its target prior to bomb release.

The AGM-130 is essentially an EGBU-15 with an AIM-7 Sparrow rocket motor strapped to its bottom, increasing the weapon's standoff range. Both the EGBU-15 and AGM-130 can only be carried on stations 2/8, and always accompanied by an AN/AXQ-14 data link pod (which occupies station 5). Due to clearance limitations, the EGBU-15/AGM-130 cannot be carried when an AIM-120 is present on the wing-mounted missile rails. An AIM-9, however, can be carried.

The CBU-87 is one of several types of cluster bombs cleared for use by the F-15E. It is a 1,000 lb, Combined Effects Munition (CEM) for use against "soft" targets. The cluster bomb's casing opens as it is dropped, releasing bomblets which then disperse, spreading the range of a single bomb. A total of 202 bomblets are loaded into each CBU-87, enabling a single payload attack against a variety of targets and a wide area of coverage. However, this wide area of coverage has sometimes resulted in inadvertent collateral damage. For this reason, "dumb" cluster bombs have largely fallen out of favor with the US military, including the F-15.

The WCMD (Wind Corrected Munitions Dispenser) program adds a tailkit to existing cluster munitions, such as the CBU-87, CBU-89, and CBU-97, resulting in the CBU-103. The WCMD tailkit assembly corrects for wind effects and errors during the weapon's ballistic fall, achieving an accuracy of within 30 feet. It is capable of delivery from medium to high altitude, allowing the delivery aircraft to remain at a safer, higher, altitude during weapons delivery. It was introduced to the F-15E in 2001 and dropped for the first time over Afghanistan.

Below-- Precise control of the bomb's "footprint" is determined by the weapons troops via knobs on the nose of the WCMD. The altitude that the bomb breaks apart and the speed at which the bomb rotates can both be adjusted to achieve the desired results.

Dumb bombs

Although the use of LDGP (Low Drag General Purpose) bombs in combat has become somewhat limited, it does still occur. They are dropped from F-15Es on targets over Iraq and Afghanistan almost daily. They are also common during peacetime training missions, either inert training rounds (with blue stripes or entire blue bodies) or live bombs (with yellow stripes around the fuse) that can be dropped over the bombing ranges to give the crews experience with live weapons. This page details the 500lb Mk. 82 Air Inflatable Retard (AIR), which has a parachute pack in the rear of the tailkit that deploys to slow the bomb's descent after drop. This allows the aircraft to escape the impact area, thus decreasing the chances of the jet being damaged by its own bomb's explosion at low altitude. Standard Mk. 82 bombs, below, are also still in use, as are heavier 2,000lb Mk. 84 bombs. However, they are less common. Several types of fuses are in use. Each has a different purpose, depending on the target.

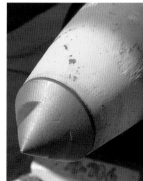

Jake Melampy

SUU-20 Bomb Dispenser

The SUU-20 is a practice bomb and rocket dispenser used for training by most USAF aircraft, including the F-15. It can carry up to six BDU-33 practice bombs at a time, ejected by a pyrotechnic charge, or four 2.75 inch rockets (although the rocket feature has been used sparingly for several years now). The Eagle can carry up to three SUU-20 dispensers at a time, on stations 2/8 and 5.

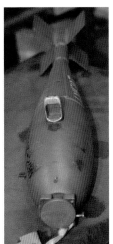

The BDU-33 is a 25 pound practice bomb used during training. It emits a puff of smoke when it impacts the ground, giving the pilot and/or ground controllers a reliable and instant indication of success. It is designed to have similar ballistic capabilites to the Mk. 82 LDGP bombs. It can be carried by nearly all tactical fighters in the USAF inventory.

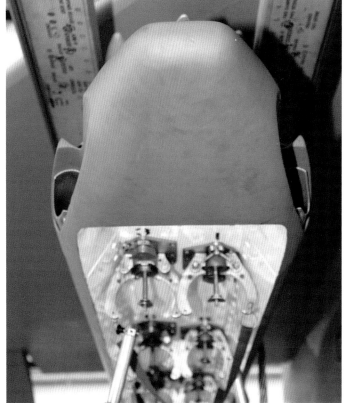

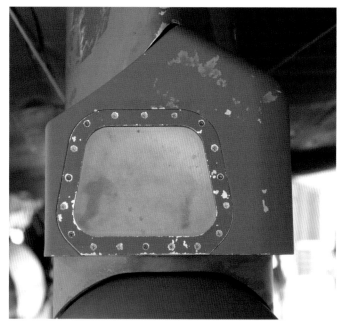

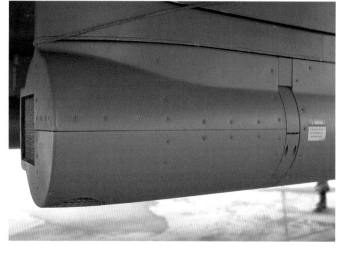

The LANTIRN (Low Altitude Navigation and Targeting Infra Red For Night) system consists of the AN/AAQ-13 navigation pod and AN/AAQ-14 targeting pods carried on specially-adapted pylons mounted to the bottom of each of the F-15E's intakes. The right side of the jet contains the navigation pod, complete with FLIR (Forward Looking Infra Red) that displays a video image of the terrain on the pilot's HUD, allowing high-speed flight at very low altitude (200ft. above ground level). The pilot can manually fly the jet using cues from the nav pod's commands on the HUD, or couple the jet's autopilot, resulting in "hands-free" flight.

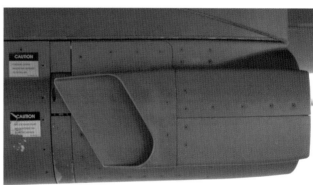

The other half of LANTIRN is the AN/AAQ-14 targeting pod, mounted underneath the jet's left intake. It is used by the Strike Eagle's Weapons Systems Officer to find and select potential targets. It can be coupled to the jet's radar or used manually by the WSO. In addition, the targeting pod contains a laser designator used to guide laser-guided bombs that detect and track the reflected laser light.

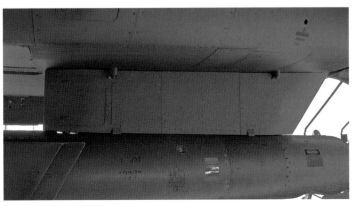

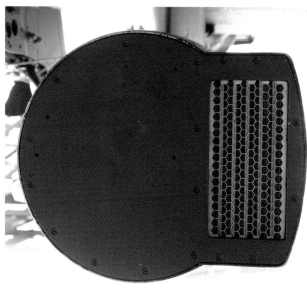

(Below) The F-15K uses a modified LANTIRN targeting pod known as Tiger Eyes. It functions essentially the same as the AN/AAQ-14, but with the added benefit of a long-range IRST (Infra Red Search and Track) similar to that found on the retired F-14D Tomcat. Mounted inegrally to the targeting pod's pylon, the IRST allows the F-15K to engage enemy aircraft at long range without using its radar system. A protective red cover is frequently in place over the IRST when the jet is parked to protect the lens.

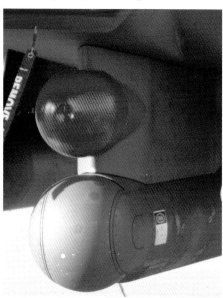

Darren Mottram

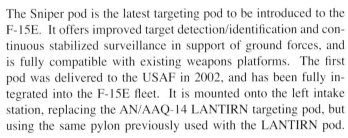

The Sniper pod is the latest targeting pod to be introduced to the F-15E. It offers improved target detection/identification and continuous stabilized surveillance in support of ground forces, and is fully compatible with existing weapons platforms. The first pod was delivered to the USAF in 2002, and has been fully integrated into the F-15E fleet. It is mounted onto the left intake station, replacing the AN/AAQ-14 LANTIRN targeting pod, but using the same pylon previously used with the LANTIRN pod.

The MXU-648 travel pod is used whenever the jet is away from its home base to carry such things as pilot's luggage, aircraft covers, extra forms, or even golf clubs and beer. Modified from surplus napalm tanks during the 1980's, many pods show heavy signs of wear and tear. However, usually at least one pod per squadron is kept for use at airshows or the personal use of the Wing and/or Squadron Commanders, and is painted and decorated accordingly. Travel pods are most often carried on the wing stations or the CFT pylons of the F-15E.

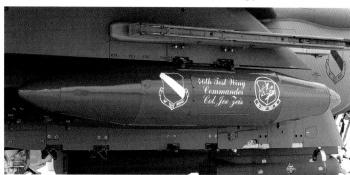

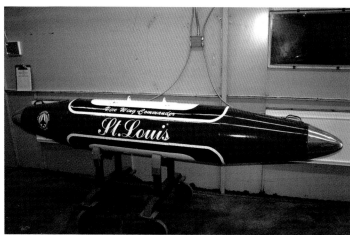

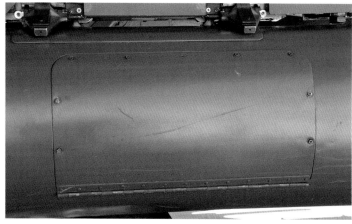

1st Fighter Wing (FF)
Langley AFB, Virginia

•27th Fighter Squadron (Spads)
   1976-1982 (F-15A/B)
   1981-2005 (F-15C/D)
•71st Fighter Squadron (Ironmen)
   1976-1982 (F-15A/B)
   1981-present (F-15C/D)
•94th Fighter Squadron (Hat in the Ring)
   1976-1983 (F-15A/B)
   1981-2005 (F-15C/D)

3rd Wing (AK)
Elmondorf AFB, Alaska

•12th Fighter Squadron (Dirty Dozen)
   2000-present (F-15C/D)
•19th Fighter Squadron (Gamecocks)
   1994-present (F-15C/D)

18th Wing (ZZ)
Kadena AB, Japan

•*12th Fighter Squadron (Dirty Dozen)*
    1979-1999 (F-15C/D)
•*44th Fighter Squadron (Vampires)*
    1980-present (F-15C/D)
•*67th Fighter Squadron (Gamecocks)*
    1979-present (F-15C/D)

21st Tactical Fighter Wing (AK)
Elmendorf AFB, Alaska

•*43rd Tactical Fighter Squadron*
    1982-1987 (F-15A/B)
    1987-1993 (F-15C/D)
•*54th Fighter Squadron*
    1987-1993 (F-15C/D)

32nd Tactical Fighter Squadron (CR)
Soesterberg AB, The Netherlands
1978-1983 (F-15A/B)
1983-1991 (F-15C/D)
1991-1993 (F-15A/B)

•*The 32TFS was under Royal Netherlands Air Force control, the only USAF squadron ever to do so.*

33rd Fighter Wing (EG)
Eglin AFB, Florida

•*58th Fighter Squadron (Gorillas)*
1979-present (F-15C/D)
•*59th Fighter Squadron (Golden Pride)*
1978-1983 (F-15A/B)
1983-1999 (F-15C/D)
•*60th Fighter Squadron (Fighting Crows)*
1978-1983 (F-15A/B)
1983-present (F-15C/D)

36th Tactical Fighter Wing (BT)
Bitburg AB, Germany

•*22nd Fighter Squadron (Stingers)*
    1977-1980 (F-15A/B)
    1980-1993 (F-15C/D)

•*53rd Fighter Squadron (Tigers)*
    1977-1981 (F-15A/B)
    1982-1993 (F-15C/D)
•*525th Fighter Squadron (Bulldogs)*
    1977-1981 (F-15A/B)
    1982-1992 (F-15C/D)

46th Test Wing (ET)
Eglin AFB, Florida

•*40th Flight Test Squadron*
    1977-2006 (F-15A/B)
    1983-present (F-15C/D)
previously 3246th Test Wing
 2347th Test Squadron

48th Fighter Wing (LN)
RAF Lakenheath, England

•*493rd Fighter Squadron (Grim Reapers)*
    1992-present (F-15C/D)

49th Tactical Fighter Wing (HO)
Holloman AFB, New Mexico

•*7th Fighter Squadron (Screamin' Demons)*
    1977-1981 (F-15A/B)
    1982-1992 (F-15C/D)
•*8th Fighter Squadron (The Black Sheep)*
    1977-1992 (F-15A/B)
•*9th Fighter Squadron (Iron Knights)*
    1977-1991 (F-15A/B)

USAF

52nd Fighter Wing (SP)
Spangdahlem AB, Germany

•53rd Fighter Squadron (Tigers)
     1993-1999 (F-15C/D)

53rd Test & Evaluation Group (OT)

•85th Test and Evaluation Squadron (Skulls)
     Eglin AFB, Florida
     1977-1982 (F-15A/B)
     1982-present (F-15C/D)

•422nd Test and Evaluation Squadron (Green Bats)
     Nellis AFB, Nevada
     1982-1989 (F-15A/B)
     1980-present (F-15C/D)

57th Wing (WA)
Nellis AFB, Nevada

•*65th Aggressors Squadron (Gomers)*
     2005-present (F-15C/D)
•*433rd Weapons Squadron (Satan's Angels)*
     1976-1999 (F-15A/B)
     1982-present (F-15C/D)

171

58th Tactical Training Wing (LA)
405th Tactical Training Wing (LA)
Luke AFB, Arizona

- 405th Training Squadron
  - 1977-1990 (F-15A/B)
- 426th Training Squadron
  - 1981-1990 (F-15A/B)
  - 1989-1990 (F-15C/D)
- 461st Training Squadron (Deadly Jesters)
  - 1977-1988 (F-15A/B))
  - 1983-1988 (F-15C/D)

- 550th Training Squadron (Silver Eagles)
  - 1977-1986 (F-15A/B)
  - 1984-1987 (F-15C/D)
- 555th Training Squadron (Triple Nickel)
  - 1974-1991 (F-15A/B)
  - 1982-1991 (F-15C/D)

The Squadrons and F-15s were transferred from the 58TTW to the 405TTW in 1979, then to the 58th Fighter wing in 1991.

325th Fighter Wing (TY)
Tyndall AFB, Florida

- 1st Fighter Squadron (Miss Fury)
  - 1984-2006 (F-15C/D)
- 2nd Fighter Squadron (American Beagle Squadron)
  - 1984-present (F-15C/D)
- 95th Fighter Squadron (Mr. Bones/Boneheads)
  - 1984-present (F-15C/D)

366th Fighter Wing (MO)
Mountain Home AFB, Idaho

- 390th Fighter Squadron (Wild Boars)
  - 1992-present (F-15C/D)

412th Test Wing (ED)
Edwards AFB, California

*previously 6510th Test Wing
  6512th Test Squadron

•415th Flight Test Squadron
        1988-1994 F-15A/B/C/D)
•445th Flight Test Squadron
        1988-2004 F-15A/B/C/D)

Dedicated Air Defense Units

5th Fighter Interceptor Squadron
Minot AFB, North Dakota

   1985 (F-15A/B)

57th Fighter Squadron (IS)
Keflavik AS, Iceland

    1985-1995 (F-15C/D)

48th Fighter Interceptor Squadron
Langley AFB, Virginia

   1982-1991 (F-15A/B)

318th Fighter Interceptor Squadron
McChord AFB, Washington

    1983-1989 (F-15A/B)

Appendix B: ANG F-15A/B/C/D Eagle Units

102nd Fighter Wing (MA)
Otis Air National Guard Base
Massachussetts ANG

•*101st Fighter Squadron*
  1987-2006 (F-15A/B)
  2006-2008 (F-15C/D)
*Victims of 2005 BRAC recommendations

104th Fighter Wing (MA)
Barnes Municipal Airport
Massachussetts ANG

•*131st Fighter Squadron*
  2007-present (F-15C/D)

116th Fighter Wing (GA)
Dobbins ARB, Georgia
Georgia ANG

•*128th Fighter Squadron*
  1986-1995 (F-15A/B)

125th Fighter Wing
Jacksonville International Airport
Florida ANG

•125th Fighter Squadron
   1995-2008 (F-15A/B)
   2005-present (F-15C/D)

131st Fighter Wing (SL)
St. Louis International Airport
Missouri ANG

•110th Fighter Squadron
   1991-2005 (F-15A/B)
   2005-2009 (F-15C/D)
*Victims of 2005 BRAC recommendations

142nd Fighter Wing
Portland International Airport
Oregon ANG

•123rd Fighter Squadron
   1988-2008 (F-15A/B)
   2005-present (F-15C/D)

154th Wing (HH)
Hickam AFB
Hawaii ANG

•199th Fighter Squadron
   1987-2007 (F-15A/B)
   2005-present (F-15C/D)

159th Fighter Wing (JZ)
NAS New Orleans JRB
Louisiana ANG

• *122nd Fighter Squadron*
  1989-2008 (F-15A/B)
  2005-present (F-15C/D)

USAF

173rd Fighter Wing
Klamath Falls
Oregon ANG

• *114th Fighter Squadron*
  1997-2007 (F-15A/B)
  2004-present (F-15C/D)

3rd Wing (AK)
Elmendorf AFB, Alaska

•*90th Fighter Squadron (Pair 'O' Dice)*
   1990-2007

4th Fighter Wing (SJ)
Seymour Johnson AFB, North Carolina

•*333rd Fighter Squadron (Lancers)*
   1994-present
•*334th Fighter Squadron (Eagles)*
   1990-present
•*335th Fighter Squadron (Chiefs)*
   1990-present
•*336th Fighter Squadron (Rocketeers)*
   1988-present

46th Test Wing (ET)
Eglin AFB, Florida

•40th Flight Test Squadron   *previously 3246th Test Wing
    1989-present   2347th Test Squadron

48th Fighter Wing (LN)
RAF Lakenheath, England

•492nd Fighter Squadron (Bolars)
    1992-present
•494th Fighter Squadron (Panthers)
    1992-present

53rd Test & Evaluation Group (OT)

•*422nd Test and Evaluation Squadron (Green Bats)*
  Nellis AFB, Nevada
  1989-present
•*85th Test and Evaluation Squadron (Skulls)*
  Eglin AFB, Florida
  1992-present

58th Fighter Wing (LA)
Luke AFB, Arizona

•*405th Training Squadron*
  1992-1994
•*461st Training Squadron (Deadly Jesters)*
  1988-1994

•*550th Training Squadron (Silver Eagles)*
  1989-1995
•*550th Training Squadron (Triple Nickel)*
  1991-1994

*Previously, the 58FW was part of the 405th Tactical Training Wing until 1991. The Wing became the 56th Fighter Wing in 1994.

57th Wing (WA)
Nellis AFB, Nevada

•*17th Weapons Squadron*
  1991-present

366th Fighter Wing (MO)
Mountain Home AFB, Idaho

•*389th Fighter Squadron (Thunderbolts)*
  2007-present
•*391st Fighter Squadron (Bold Tigers)*
  1992-present

412th Test Wing (ED)
Edwards AFB, California
**previously 6510th Test Wing*

•*415th Flight Test Squadron*
  1988-1994
•*445th Flight Test Squadron*
  1994-2004

69 Tayeset (69 Squadron)
Hatzerim Air Base

•*F-15I Ra'am*
   1998-present

106 Tayeset (106 Squadron)
Tel Nof Air Base

•*F-15B/C/D (Baz)*
   1982-present

133 Tayeset (133 Squadron)
Tel Nof Air Base

•*F-15A/B (Baz)*
   1977-present
•*F-15C/D (Baz)*
   1982-present

No. 5 Squadron
King Fahd AB, Taif

•*F-15C/D*
  1981-present

No. 6 Squadron
King Khaled AB, Khamis Mushayt

•*F-15C/D*   *F-15S*
  1981-present   *1998-present*

No. 13 Squadron
King Abdul Aziz AB, Dhahran

•*F-15C/D*
  1981-present

No. 42 Squadron
King Khaled AB, Khamis Mushayt

•*F-15C/D*
  1991-present

No. 55 Squadron
King Khaled AB, Khamis Mushayt

•*F-15S*
  1995-present

No. 92 Squadron
King Abdul Aziz AB, Dhahran

•*F-15S*
  1996-present

Hiko Kyodo-tai (Tactical Fighter Training Group)
Nyutabaru Air Base

•*F-15J/DJ*
  1990-present
  * *Japanese Aggressor Squadron*

Hiko Kaihatsu Jikken-dan (Air Development and Test Group)
Gifu Air Base

•*F-15J/DJ*   *1982-present*

Dai 2 Koku-dan (2nd Air Wing)
Chitose Air Base

•*Dai 201 Hiko-Tai (201 Squadron)*
  1986-present
•*Dai 203 Hiko-Tai (203 Squadron)*
  1983-present

Dai 5 Koku-dan (5th Air Wing)
Nyutabaru Air Base

•*Dai 202 Hiko-Tai (202 Squadron)*
  1981-present

Dai 6 Koku-dan (6th Air Wing)
Komatsu Air Base

•*Dai 303 Hiko-Tai (303 Squadron)*   •*Dai 306 Hiko-Tai (306 Squadron)*
  1986-present   *1995-present*

184

Appendix F: Japan Air Self-Defense Force

Dai 7 Koku-dan (7th Air Wing)
Hyakuri Air Base

- *Dai 204 Hiko-Tai (204 Squadron)*
    1984-present
- *Dai 305 Hiko-Tai (305 Squadron)*
    1993-present

Dai 8 Koku-dan (8th Air Wing)
Tsuiki Air Base

- *Dai 304 Hiko-Tai (304 Squadron)*
    1990-present

Darren Mottram

Appendix G: Republic of Korea Air Force/ Han Guk Gong Gun

11th Fighter Wing
Daegu Air Base

- *102nd Fighter Squadron*
    F-15K 2006-present
- *122nd Fighter Squadron*
    F-15K 2005-present

Appendix H: Republic of Singapore Air Force

At the time of writing (Summer 2008), the RSiAF has placed an order for the Boeing F-15SG, based on the F-15E. Deliveries are expected to commence in late 2008 and 2009.

Building an Eagle model? Chances are, Afterburner Decals has something that will grab your attention. In a short time, they've risen to the top of the hill in the Aviation Decal industry, and these Eagle sheets are one of the many reasons why. Check them out at WWW.AFTERBURNERDECALS.COM!

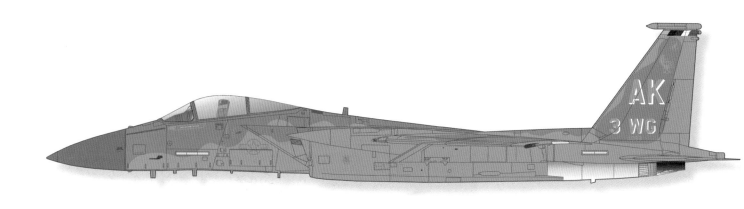

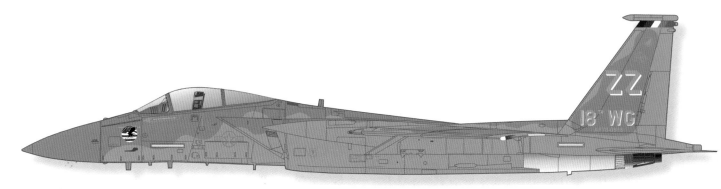

Eagle Wing Kings #1 #48-019

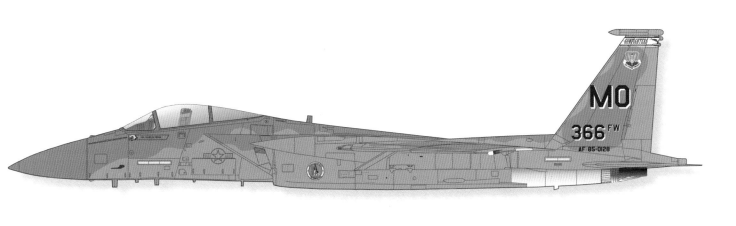

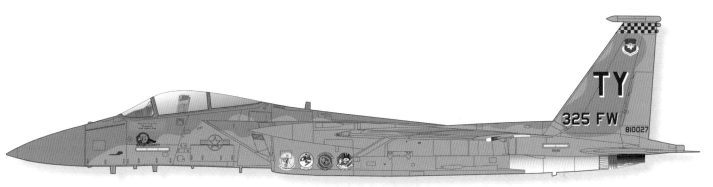

Eagle Wing Kings #2 #48-021

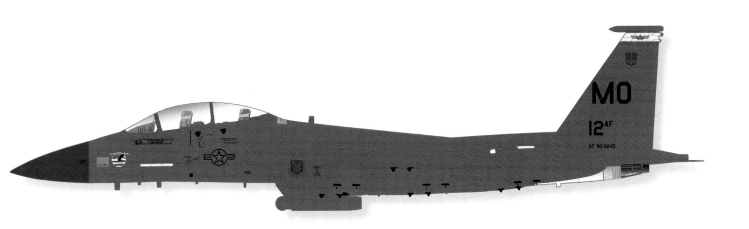

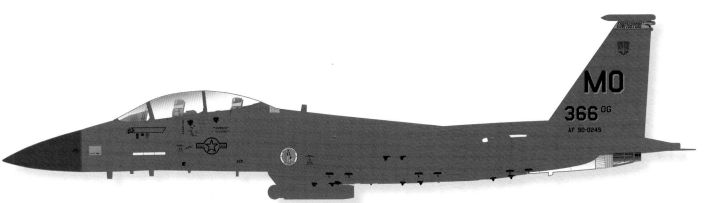

Strike Eagle Gunfighters #48-031

187

Also from the author:

The Viper Story, Part I: F-16s of the Air National Guard
ISBN # 978-0-9795064-0-6

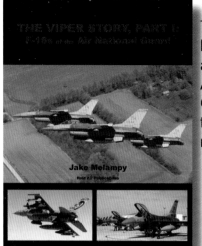

The first of a 4-part series covering the F-16 in service with the USAF, this book features 247 pages of full-color, high-quality images. The images are paired with text to tell the complete story of the Viper as flown by the ANG. Each unit to have ever flown the type since the first jet arrived in Guard service in 1983 is covered, along with photos taken during wartime, mission markings, special/anniversary paintschemes, nose art, and more.

"Jake Melampy's book on the F-16 in the Air National Guard (ANG) has to be, in my opinion, the most comprehensive book on the subject to date, even more so than any magazine or journal that I have seen. This book will have appeal for any enthusiast, military historian, or to any one who is around the F-16."

--Jon Somerville, www.f-16.net editor

The Modern Viper Guide: The F-16C/D Exposed
ISBN # 978-0-9795064-1-3

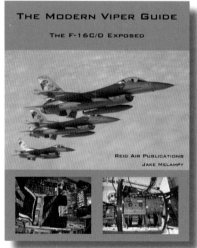

The Modern Viper Guide is the most comprehensive detail-type book on the F-16 ever released. Working with F-16 pilots and crewchiefs, this book explores each F-16 production Block with textual and photographic descriptions of each similarity and difference, from Block 25 righ through Block 52. Special emphasis is placed on modern upgrade programs such as CUPID and CCIP, along with modern weapons, ie: LITENING, Sniper, GBU-31 JDAM, WCMD, etc. An absolute "must-have" for the enthusiast or anyone wishing to build a modern, detailed, model of the F-16! 136 pages, full color throughout.

The Modern Hog Guide: The A-10 Warthog Exposed
ISBN # 978-0-9795064-2-0

Following on from the success of The Modern Viper Guide, The Modern Hog Guide explores the A-10 inside and out. Again working with crewchiefs and pilots of the real aircraft, The Modern Hog Guide brings the reader up to date with modern upgrades, service-life extension programs, and weapons. Over 700 photos of the cockpit (all versions, from pre-LASTE Desert Storm era to the "glass cockpit" of the A-10C), airframe, engines, weapons, gun, avionics, etc. This is the ONLY A-10 book you'll ever need if you're wishing to build a scale model of the Hog! 120 pages, full color throughout.